HISTORY OF STAND-UP

FROM MARK TWAIN TO DAVE CHAPPELLE

ALSO BY WAYNE FEDERMAN

Maravich

The Authorized Biography of Pistol Pete

With Marshall Terrill

HISTORY OF STAND-UP

FROM MARK TWAIN TO DAVE CHAPPELLE

WAYNE FEDERMAN

Independent Artists Media

Beverly Hills New York Silver Spring

Cover designed by Andrew Steven
Book designed by Brandon Mullins

Printed in United States of America

Library of Congress Control Number: 2021904374

Federman, Wayne
History of stand-up: from Mark Twain to Dave Chappelle by Wayne Federman

Includes bibliographical references and index
1. Comedians – United States 2. Title

First Printing 2021
10 9 8 7 6 5 4 3 2 1

Published by
Independent Artists Media
9190 West Olympic Blvd.
Beverly Hills, CA 90212
Ftrain@me.com
www.WayneFederman.com

For Stand-Up Comedians
And their Fans
Yesterday, Today, Tomorrow

CONTENTS

Introduction

The aim of this book is to provide a brief, and breezy, overview of how stand-up comedy developed in the United States.

The contents were mostly culled from four sources:

1. The stand-up history and performance class I currently teach at USC.
2. Multiple articles I have written on comedy, primarily for *Vulture*.
3. My *History of Stand-Up* podcast with Andrew Steven.
4. Thirty-eight years (and counting) working clubs and theaters as a comedian.

Before the Covid-19 virus shut down the entertainment industry in March 2020, the US was experiencing its second comedy boom. And it was massive.

One could see live stand-up in bars, clubs, house shows, alt rooms, theaters, and arenas. You could watch it on your screen of choice. It was in your news feed. You could hear stand-up comics on a multitude of satellite radio channels, podcasts, and audio-streaming services. You could easily purchase entire comedy albums or individual tracks. *Forbes* magazine published an annual highest-earning comedians list while *Billboard* magazine had its own dedicated comedy album sales chart. The internet brought comedians and their superfans closer than ever before. You could even study comedy history, theory, and practice at universities... and be awarded a degree.

So how did this all happen?

Before we begin to answer that question, I wanted to share a few thoughts about stand-up in general.

Stand-up comedy is primarily a generational art form. With very few exceptions, it doesn't age too well. Joke construction, cultural references, jargon, taboos, use of profanity, and acceptable subject matter continually change as each new wave of comedians take the field.

The harsh fact is that many comics that were once hailed as hilariously cutting-edge can, in just a few decades, seem out-of-touch, corny, or simply unfunny to current audiences.

It's just the nature of the art form.

The history of stand-up provides a fascinating study of lineage. Almost all comics are influenced and inspired by the performers that preceded them. Icons Richard Pryor and Robert Klein produced scores of comics who copped their style. But some comedians drew their inspiration from more obscure performers.

- An English vaudevillian "Griff" inspired Fred Allen.
- Frank Fay lit the stand-up fire for Bob Hope.
- Jean Carroll delighted a young Lily Tomlin.
- Herb Shriner was a hero to Mort Sahl.
- Wally Boag captivated and inspired Steve Martin.

Stand-up's history also parallels the evolution of modern technologies. Comedians, like pornographers, are early and nimble adaptors. They are ready to pivot as each new invention or innovation presents fresh opportunities. The list includes audio recordings, stage microphones, radio, movies, television, record albums, cable TV, home video, premium channels, e-mail, online videos, podcasting, digital downloads, social media, smart phones, and now streaming on Twitch, Zoom, Facebook, YouTube, Instagram, and (audio only) Clubhouse. The ultimate impact of the pandemic on stand-up comedy remains unknown. Are we entering a post-stand-up era? Will 2020-21 be seen as the *inflection point* where everything changed? Time will eventually answer those questions but now might be a good moment to take a look back... and see how we got here.

However, before we embark, it would be difficult to summarize stand-up's history without including several comedians whose offstage behavior has ranged from problematic to detestable to illegal. I hope reading their names won't ruin this journey.

So, let's go back. All the way to the 1850s...

Will Rogers "The Cherokee Kid"

1

THE FOUR FOREFATHERS

I study carefully the acoustics of each theatre I appear in. There is always one particular spot on the stage from which the voice carries better, more clearly and easily than from any other. I make it my business to find that spot before the first performance, and once I find it, I stick to it like a postage stamp.

— Bert Williams

WHO WAS the first comedian? Who was the needy extrovert that started this whole thing? Much like the origin of the universe, the answer is unknowable.

Who can say with any certainty that there weren't funny hunters who acted-out their tribe's unsuccessful attempt to kill a woolly mammoth? We know *some* human beings have been trying to make *other* humans laugh for thousands of years before there was a Phyllis Diller. It's always been a part of human culture.

So where to start? I'm choosing to begin this historical journey by spotlighting the four men I consider to be the forefathers of American stand-up comedy.

1. Artemus Ward
2. Mark Twain
3. Bert Williams
4. Will Rogers

Now to be precise, the term stand-up wasn't coined until around 1947, so none of these gentlemen (all born in the 1800s) were literal stand-up comedians. But all of them, at some point, performed, on stage, in that style.

And none of them made it past the 10th grade.

There was no Comedy Store, Improv, Caroline's, or Comedy Cellar for comics to showcase and develop their craft. Instead, they came up in the "show business" of their time: taverns, minstrel shows, circuses, saloons, dime museums, lecture circuits, fairs (city, county, state, and world), riverboats, honky-tonks, tent shows, Wild West shows, medicine shows, amusement parks, and then eventually vaudeville, burlesque, tab shows, Broadway, variety revues, network radio, silent films, records, and sound movies.

All four of our comedic forefathers were so popular that they were able to successfully tour outside the United States.

I have studied comedians and comedy history since I was a teenager and had not heard of Artemus Ward (born 1834) until fellow comedian, author, and comedy historian Ritch Shydner opened my eyes to this trailblazer.

Ward's actual name is Charles F. Browne (yep, Charlie Brown was arguably the first American stand-up). Browne was working as a newspaperman at the *Cleveland Plain-Dealer* when, in January 1858, he began publishing humorous letters, with purposely misspelled words, and signed them "Artemus Ward."

Rather quickly the letters found an appreciative audience. They were soon reprinted in hundreds of newspapers around the country, enabling the character Artemus Ward to reach a massive audience. (Back then popular columns were permitted to be copied into any newspaper without permission or financial compensation.)

His legend spread like a prairie fire and in just a few months

Artemus Ward was known across America. That comedic accomplishment alone would be noteworthy.

But what happened next was even more incredible.

One of Browne's reporting responsibilities was covering the local entertainment scene, including the minstrel shows that visited Cleveland.

* Note: More about the minstrel tradition and its influence on modern American stand-up later on.

Browne was shocked when one of the minstrel performers began reciting a comedy bit lifted from a recent Artemus Ward newspaper "letter." The minstrel was getting consistent laughs and Browne's mood changed from shock to curiosity as he realized that his work could be repurposed from newsprint to the stage.

After the show, Browne began to wonder if he could possibly re-invent himself as a stage performer. After all, he had created this Artemus Ward character.

And, incredibly, that's exactly what happened.

The shy Browne bought a book on public speaking, quit his newspaper gig, moved to NYC, wrote for *Vanity Fair* (then a comedy magazine), published a compilation of his old Artemus Ward letters/columns, and tried his luck on the stage.

Browne's venues of choice were small theaters and halls that booked serious lecturers. At that time lectures were an increasingly popular form of "elevated" entertainment that sought to promote knowledge, literacy, and virtue. It was a thriving 19th century version of adult education that appealed to a growing, aspirational middle-class citizenry. Experts crisscrossed the country pontificating on an array of topics. It was called the Lyceum Movement and these live presentations were like a short MasterClass – or a very long Ted Talk.

The first Artemus Ward comedy lecture was given on Tuesday, November 26, 1861. It was entitled "Babes in the Wood," and featured Ward speaking alone on stage for one-hour and twenty minutes. And throughout the entire presentation he *never addressed* the lecture's topic. And that was his hook. Ward, in a controlled deadpan style, cleverly avoided the subject of "Babes in The Wood," and instead explored multiple comedic tangents.

Ward's comedy act was a sensation and some historians point to his breakthrough concept as the birth of stand-up comedy.

Hoping to capitalize on the national notoriety from his old newspaper columns and new book (even President Lincoln was a fan), Ward eventually toured his comedy lecture throughout the country. It proved extremely lucrative, with tickets going for fifty cents or a dollar. For a single performance in San Francisco he grossed over $1,500 – that would be about $38,000 in 2021. His peak salary back at the newspaper in Cleveland was $14 *a week* – ($362 in 2021).

Ward's legend spread to Europe, so, in 1866, he brought his comedy lecture to England and set up a residency at the Egyptian Hall in Piccadilly. There he played to packed houses and critical praise.

England is also where he dropped dead of tuberculosis. He was just 32 and had been touring as Artemus for five years.

But three years before Artemus Ward's untimely death, he had a fateful interaction with an aspiring writer who would later transform both American literature and American humor. His name was Samuel Clemens.

Clemens was a 29-year-old staff writer for a Nevada Territory newspaper when, in December of 1863, Artemus Ward rolled into town to perform his famous lecture. Watching Ward on stage, Clemens was astonished by the number of laughs Ward evoked and was captivated by his mock-serious, joke telling style.

The two hit it off immediately and Ward spent his whole

Christmas vacation hanging out with Clemens along with some other local newspapermen. It would be the only time that these two comedy pioneers were in each other's company. But Clemens never forgot those days and the impact of Ward's deadpan style.

This passage is from Clemens' 1897 book, *How to Tell A Story*:

"The humorous story is told gravely; the teller does his best to conceal the fact that he even dimly suspects that there is anything funny about it... Artemus Ward used that trick a good deal; then when the belated audience presently caught the joke he would look up with innocent surprise, as if wondering what they had found to laugh at."

The Mark Twain lectures, which were predominantly comedic (with some moments of melancholy), were greeted with great enthusiasm wherever he traveled. Bolstered by his acclaimed books and newspaper articles, he was able to successfully tour the United States, Canada, England, Australia, Italy, Germany, New Zealand, South Africa, Austria, India, and Hungary.

All of these shows took place before the existence of air travel.

Here are Twain's U.S. tour dates for the month of December, 1869. (Special thanks to Barbara Schmidt for this information.)

December 1 - Brooklyn Library Society, Brooklyn, New York
December 3 - Collingwood's Opera House, Poughkeepsie, New York
December 6 - Beecher's Plymouth Church, Brooklyn, New York
December 7 - Academy of Music, Philadelphia, Pennsylvania
December 8 - Lincoln Hall, Washington, D.C.
December 9 - Germantown, Pennsylvania
December 10 - Methodist Church, Mount Vernon, New York

December 11 - Town Hall, West Meriden, Connecticut
December 13 - Union Hall, New Britain, Connecticut
December 14 - Warren, Massachusetts
December 15 - Armory Hall, Pawtucket, Rhode Island
December 16 - Rumford Institute, Waltham, Massachusetts
December 20 - Canton, Massachusetts
December 21 - Hudson, Massachusetts
December 22 - Mercantile Library, Portland, Maine
December 23 - Town Hall, Rockport, Massachusetts
December 24 - Slatersville, Rhode Island
December 27 - Music Hall, New Haven, Connecticut
December 28 - Taylor Hall, Trenton, New Jersey
December 29 - Opera House, Newark, New Jersey
December 30 - Landmesser Hall, Wilkes-Barre, Pennsylvania
December 31 - Opera House, Williamsport, Pennsylvania

Eighty-eight years after his death, the Kennedy Center began awarding an annual *Mark Twain Prize*. It was presented to individuals who have made a significant *comedic* impact on American culture.

Richard Pryor was the first honoree.

The other stand-up comedians who have received the Mark Twain Prize are Jonathan Winters, Jay Leno, Bob Newhart, Lily Tomlin, Bill Cosby (later rescinded), Billy Crystal, Whoopi Goldberg, Steve Martin, George Carlin, Eddie Murphy, Ellen DeGeneres, David Letterman, and Dave Chappelle.

There are no audio recordings of Mark Twain's voice and he never acted in films or in the legitimate theater. But that was certainly not the case with our third forefather of stand-up comedy: Bert Williams.

Bert Williams excelled in multiple arenas of show business that are very familiar to present-day audiences, including movies, records, and Broadway. In fact, he recorded numerous hit comedy songs for Columbia, a record label that still exists in 2021.

Some refer to Bert Williams as America's first black superstar comedian. Although telling jokes was just part of his repertoire. His most famous onstage bit was a brilliant pantomime of a poker game. The magnitude of Williams' talents, especially during a time when big-time show business routinely excluded most black entertainers, made his achievements both remarkable and historic.

Born in 1874, Williams began developing his comic sensibility the same way that hundreds, if not thousands, of 20th and 21st century comedians have... in school.

The classroom was a comedy workshop for Williams. He had a talent for impressions and dialects and was a curious observer of his classmates and teachers. He was also fascinated by barnyard animals, birds, and insects. He loved the structure of jokes that he learned from the Almanac.

Williams got the show business bug and dropped out of school in the 10th grade.

There were no reputable comedy lecture tours for Williams. He began his show biz journey at the very bottom, as a *barker* for a medicine show. Barkers were performers who stood outside a venue/tent and attempted to lure customers into the show. ("Barking" outside comedy clubs still exists for aspiring stand-up comics in the 21st century.)

Medicine shows were circus-like traveling troupes that crisscrossed the USA. They mixed a presentation of fast-paced variety acts (singers, dancers, comedians, fortune tellers, magicians) with an effective sales pitch that hawked an array of "patented" pharmaceutical tonics, miracle elixirs, potions, and oils (like from a snake). Both the parents and grandparents of silent film legend Buster Keaton worked medicine shows. As did escape artist Harry Houdini and comedian Red Skelton. This is where the journey began for Bert Williams. But his career was about to change dramatically. In 1893, Williams got hired to perform as part of a small minstrel troupe in San Francisco.

Quick educational sidebar.

To better understand the roots of modern stand-up, I cannot ignore (as much as I'd like to) the legacy and influence of the minstrel show. So here goes.

Minstrel shows consisted of white actors, comics, dancers, musicians, and singers who smeared their faces with a concoction of burned cork and petroleum jelly into an exaggerated "blackface" theatrical mask.

This performance style began to gain popularity in the late 1820s in the tough Bowery district of New York City, appealing to lower class and working class immigrants. The ebullient songs and comedy-dancing of these black-faced performers stood in sharp contrast to the more delicate hymns, classical, and parlor music favored by New York's middle and upper class.

The minstrel show evolved in myriad ways, but the primary comedic aesthetic centered around dehumanizing, demeaning, and racist characterizations of African Americans. Again, this all began when owning slaves was still legal in about half the country. But despite the racism at the core of these performances, by the mid-1800s, American minstrel shows were all the rage.

New minstrel companies sprung up across the country and troupes even toured the world to great acclaim. No one had experienced anything quite like it. England's Queen Victoria (of

"Victorian Age" fame) reportedly had a grand time watching a traveling minstrel show from the USA.

The minstrel show was an original American theatrical innovation and a popular cultural export. It was a preview of other home-grown Americana that sparked international fascination like jazz, Hollywood films, rock and roll, blue jeans, basketball, hip-hop culture, and fast food.

But, for the purpose of this book, minstrelsy's foundational connection to stand-up comedy is found in three distinct ways.

1. When the minstrel show became more formalized, the show would feature two "end-men." These were comics who would fire off a succession of insults, puns, malapropisms, word plays, and jokes utilizing a set-up/punchline formula that helped blaze the path for modern-day joke construction. Also, back-and-forth repartee between the end-man and the emcee (called the interlocutor) opened the door to verbal comedy teams.

2. As each troupe entered a new city, the minstrels would cleverly insert local references of city politicians, business leaders, or wealthy families into their set routines. This helped popularize both comedy improvisation along with the tradition of satirizing the powerful, wealthy, and influential.

3. And, perhaps most importantly, midway through the show one performer would present a comedic "stump speech" based on a subject (usually politics) which was primarily a straight-ahead, first-person presentation. These stump speeches were a precursor of modern comedians who stood alone on stage and directly addressed the crowd.

Back to Bert Williams.

In 1893, according to Camille Forbes' biography, *Introducing Bert Williams,* Williams got hired as an end-man for a company called *Martin and Selig's Mastodon Minstrels.* This small minstrel troupe was diverse: five white, four African American, and one Mexican American performer. Williams was paid $7 a week.

It was the first time that Williams performed in blackface. He was following in the footsteps of other popular African American blackface minstrels of the day like Tom McIntosh, Sam Lucas, and the then-legendary Billy Kersands.

The Martin and Selig minstrel gig altered the course of Williams' professional life because it afforded him the opportunity to work with another gifted entertainer in the troupe, George Walker. The two had great comedic chemistry and soon they decided to leave the minstrel show, combine forces, and head out on their own. It turned out to be a smart move.

Over the next sixteen years, the comedy team of Williams & Walker became a ground-breaking show business force. They were featured in the first Broadway musical written and performed by African Americans (to be precise, Bert Williams was born in the Bahamas), they popularized the Cake Walk dance craze, they performed for the King of England, and they became the first black entertainers to record their voices for a major record company, the Victor Talking Machine Company (later to be RCA Victor).

In 1909, George Walker fell ill and was forced into early retirement. Bert Williams soldiered on and, as a solo act, further elevated his legendary status. He became a featured comedian in the prestigious New York revue, *The Ziegfeld Follies.* Before Bert Williams, the Follies were all-white productions.

Williams also toured the US in original stage musicals; he

wrote, directed, and starred in short silent films for Biograph Studios; and he headlined big time vaudeville where he was known as "the greatest and most original comedian in the world."

Bert Williams' act consisted of songs, dance, pantomime, and several comedy stories – which he referred to as his "lies." He closed most personal appearances with his signature song, "Nobody." The song amplified his Jonah Man onstage character, a poor soul who was beaten down by a never ending string of bad luck.

That song became the first pre-1920 recording selected into the Grammy Hall Of Fame. In October 2000, ninety-five years after Bert Williams first composed it, Johnny Cash released his version of "Nobody."

In 1917, at the New Amsterdam Theater in NYC, the newest edition of the *Ziegfeld Follies* opened. Performing that night, along with dozens of dazzling showgirls, were comedy performers W.C. Fields, Eddie Cantor, Bert Williams, Fanny Brice, and our fourth stand-up originator... Will Rogers.

Will Rogers was born in Indian Territory (now Oklahoma) in 1879. He once joked that his ancestors did not come over on the Mayflower but they certainly "met the boat." Of all his many show business achievements, Rogers is still revered and honored as the original trailblazer of topical, political humor.

"I'm not a member of any organized political party. I'm a Democrat."

Comedians that stand on stage, or in broadcast studios, and generate laughs based on "today's news" are part of this tradition. Performers like Bob Hope, Mort Sahl, Dick Gregory,

Johnny Carson, Mark Russell, Jay Leno, David Letterman, Will Durst, Jon Stewart, Stephen Colbert, Samantha Bee, Bill Maher, John Oliver, Amber Ruffin, and forty-six years of SNL Weekend Update anchors – all work in the comedic shadow of Will Rogers.

In 1902, Rogers began his unlikely show business ascent in, of all places, South Africa (then known as the Cape Colonies) when he was hired as "lasso expert" for *Texas Jack's Wild West Show and Dramatic Company*. He billed himself as the Cherokee Kid. Rogers was a Native American who played a cowboy.

Capitalizing on the larger-than-life mythology of the American frontier, Wild West shows were circus-inspired exhibitions that thrilled and amazed patrons in multiple countries. They featured the usual western-based stunts you'd expect from such a production: horseback trick riders, sharp shooters, bucking broncos, buffalo racing, cowboy vs. Indian reenactments, and lassoing demonstrations. But they also included variety acts like singers, clowns, contortionists, trapeze artists, jugglers, and acrobats. Some of the larger Wild West companies even featured a traveling zoo.

Although Will Rogers didn't speak during his lassoing demonstration, he credited his Texas Jack residency with teaching him the basics of showmanship: how to capture and hold the attention of a crowd, build anticipation, and produce a satisfying conclusion.

After just nine months touring with Texas Jack, Will Rogers departed South Africa with something extremely valuable... an act.

He eventually landed in NYC, hoping to break into vaudeville. His act was categorized as "dumb," which in show business jargon meant: no stage talking. He had only specific music cues for the house band and then, quite by accident, started getting laughs by explaining his rope-twirling tricks. New York crowds were immediately tickled by his southwestern drawl and his ability to turn any onstage miscue into a self-deprecating throwaway.

Through the years, Rogers put more comedy-philosophy into the act and less rope-trickery.

"We have the best congress that money can buy."

It's ironic that this bashful roper, who initially wouldn't dare speak onstage, transformed himself into a verbal comedy legend – all delivered in his aww-shucks, country-boy, gum-chewing style.

In the spring of 1916, the Friars Club, a show business fraternity, took a massive variety show out on the road for a multi-city fund-raising tour. It was entitled *The Friars All Star Frolic*. This original production under the direction of George M. Cohan had a huge cast and featured many popular comedians, including Julius Tannen, Frank Tinney, and Will Rogers. The third stop of the tour was the Academy of Music Theater in Baltimore, Maryland.

What made the Baltimore show unique was that the crowd included President Woodrow Wilson – who had driven up from D.C.

For Will Rogers it was a nerve-wracking night since he had a number of wisecracks about the commander-in-chief.

So, on May 30, 1916, for the first time in American history, a political comic delivered jokes about the President to the President.

Over the last twenty years of his career Will Rogers blossomed into a beloved and revered American folk hero. Besides his vaudeville, *Ziegfeld Follies*, and Broadway successes; Rogers made records, broadcast a weekly radio show, lectured across the country, wrote a wildly popular syndicated newspaper column (that were later compiled into best-selling books), organized hundreds of benefits, completed three world tours, and starred in over fifty feature films.

"I'm not a real movie star. I've still got the same wife I started out with twenty-eight years ago."

Then, in one horrific moment, it was all over.

On August 15th, 1935, Will Rogers died in a plane crash in Alaska. The moment so devastated the country that all federal buildings lowered their flags to half-mast. On the day of his funeral both NBC and CBS halted broadcasting, while over 12,000 movie theaters ceased projecting their films for "two minutes of silence."

One year before his shocking death, Rogers became the first comedian to host the Academy Awards ceremony. That booking opened the door to a bucket-list gig that comedians have coveted until 2018, when Kevin Hart backed out after some members of the Motion Picture Academy found a few of his past Twitter comments offensive.

The list of comics who have hosted, or co-hosted, the Oscars since Will Rogers kicked off the tradition in 1934 are George Jessel, Bob Burns, Bob Hope, Jack Benny, Jerry Lewis, Mort Sahl, Alan King, Richard Pryor, Johnny Carson, Robin Williams, Billy Crystal, Whoopi Goldberg, David Letterman, Steve Martin, Chris Rock, Jon Stewart, and Ellen DeGeneres.

And there you have it. These four gentlemen – Artemus Ward, Mark Twain, Bert Williams, and Will Rogers – provided the foundational DNA of modern stand-up comedy. Our journey continues with the awesome rise of a powerful cutthroat industry that modernized and corporatized American show business.

And it had a fancy French name: vaudeville.

2

VAUDEVILLE AND BURLESQUE

In vaudeville I used to come out in one. Do about twelve minutes.
And just murder the audience.

— Bob Hope

VAUDEVILLE was a family-friendly variety show with an emphasis on variety. Audiences would be entertained by a carefully constructed bill of unrelated acts, typically around nine. The biggest draw on the bill, whose name had the largest font on posters and ads, was the headliner.

At its peak, from 1900-1925, vaudeville was the epicenter of show business in the USA. There were more than 3,000 theaters that employed well over 20,000 performers each year.

Vaudeville grew out of the wild, rowdy, and alcohol-drenched variety shows of the mid-to-late 1800s. It found its brand and *massive financial windfall* when it pivoted to squeaky-clean entertainment suitable for gentleman, ladies, and even children. The operative word at the time was "polite."

Tony Pastor, the so-called "father of vaudeville," was an empresario who insisted that nothing *close* to an obscenity would ever be uttered on his stage. Profane, sexually suggestive, or vulgar expressions could get a comedian immediately fired. No "hells," "damns," or even "slobs." And no politics. Performers worked within oppressive Sunday School level speech codes.

Ironically, inside that hyper-strict environment, is where stand-up comedy began evolving.

Vaudeville showcased singers, dancers, musicians, comedy teams, contortionists, jugglers, animal acts, gun spinners, quick-change artists, impressionists, cyclists, whistlers, billiard trick-shooters, sketch performers, family acts, puppeteers, one-act plays, acrobats, trapeze artists, orators, mimes, actors, clowns, school-room acts, female impersonators, magicians, escape artists, ventriloquists, cowboys, and plate spinners. Among this smorgasbord of specialty acts was the *comedy monologist*, an early incarnation of the stand-up comic.

Monologists were in demand in part because they performed at the very front lip of the stage, the area between the main curtain and the footlights. It was called performing "in one." These acts allowed time for stagehands to quietly swap-out some scenery or set up some special theatrical rigging.

The biggest stars in vaudeville were not the *in one* monologists. But their day was coming.

Vaudeville was set up like modern professional baseball. There were the major leagues, referred to as big-time, and there were the minor leagues, known as small-time and even small small-time.

Playing big-time vaudeville meant you were most likely touring, with a secure multi-week contract, on one of two major theater chains: the Keith-Albee circuit or the Orpheum circuit. Keith-Albee controlled most of the big-time houses east of the Mississippi River while the Orpheum circuit presided over the rest of the country – as well as large swaths of Canada.

These corporations booked thousands of crowd-pleasing acts into opulent, stunning theaters that featured state-of-the-art acoustics. Performers in big-time vaudeville usually performed only twice a day, a matinee and an evening show.

Headliners in big-time vaudeville could pocket $2,500 per

week. As a point of comparison, the average salary of an American worker in 1920 was just shy of $3,300 per year. The availability of railroad travel made the whole enterprise economically feasible.

Eventually, the Keith-Albee circuit and the Orpheum circuit merged creating a super powerful entity that controlled both the big-time theaters and the booking offices. Local theater managers would carefully watch and grade each act and deliver reports back to the home office in New York City.

After opening night, a comedian might receive a blue envelope containing a list of any offensive material. If that material wasn't immediately removed from the act, the comedian would be removed from the show. Since then, bookers, agents, and journalists have referred to acts that use onstage profanity as working "blue."

However, conditions were entirely different in small-time vaudeville. On the plus side there were several well-managed theater chains (Loews, Pantages, Sullivan and Considine, Sheedy, Gus Sun) and multiple relatively plush independent houses. But small-time vaudeville could mean extremely sketchy performing venues. You could be doing your act – not in a theater – but in a cramped restaurant below a bowling alley.

One of the harshest insults you could hurl at a fellow vaudeville comic was to call them "small-time."

The accommodations in the dregs of small-time were often pitiful, getting paid was not guaranteed, and the performers worked much harder. Unlike those fancy *two-a-day* vaudevillians, small-timers were contracted for up to six shows a day. And there was even a showtime strategy called "continuous vaudeville" where customers could arrive at any time and stay as long as they pleased. The shows would start up around noon and just roll over and over until 10:30pm.

Also, to save money and aggravation, small-time vaudeville

houses began adding short films to their lineup. These silent "flickers" were just an amusing novelty back in 1900. But eventually these *novelties* would grow in both stature and artistic innovation – until their popularity would one day help smother vaudeville.

At the turn of the 20th century, the goal of every comedian was to make it up the ladder into big-time vaudeville. Despite grinding it out year after year, most performers never got close. Several tasted the big-time, couldn't sustain it, and were sent back to the minors. It was a cutthroat enterprise; and Keith-Orpheum managers would blacklist comedians if they dared play on a competing circuit. Many performers had to change their names to try and navigate the dangerous waters.

So, what sort of acts did these vaudeville comedians present? Well, at the outset (late 1800s) the overwhelming majority of comics based their act on exaggerated melting-pot ethnic and racial stereotypes such as Irish, Black, Scottish, German (also known as Dutch), Jewish (Hebrew), and Italian. And to a lesser extent Chinese, French, Mexican, and Swedish.

Those early comedians also adopted regional and social stereotypes like the tramp, the Indian, the rural cracker, the college boy, the western cowboy, and the wry New England/Yankee observer.

A clear example of early vaudeville-era comedy stereotypes can be seen in the ethnic underpinnings of film comedy legends, the Marx Brothers.

- Groucho was originally based on a *German* dialect character.
- Harpo, replete with red fright wig, grew out of an *Irish* character he had created named Patsy Brannigan.

- And Chico, with his pointy Borsellino hat, was straight-up old-school *Italian*.

Eventually Catholic organizations along with other ethnic, religious, and racial leagues began complaining to vaudeville theater managers about what they perceived as derogatory onstage portrayals. Organized pressure to eliminate racial and ethnic stereotypes began way back in 1905.

Protesting against comedians is not a recent development in America.

Another example of early vaudeville ethnic humor was the comedy team of Weber & Fields. In the late 1880s, Joe Weber and Lew Fields (still in their teens) found comedy gold when they added padding under their outfits, applied makeup, and began portraying a pair of German American immigrants trying to navigate the ins-and-outs of their new country.

Weber & Fields masterfully fused two pillars of comedy: physical and verbal. They brutally hit each other throughout the presentation. They discovered that the harder the force of the blow – the bigger the laughs. The two also verbally sparred, completely mangling the English language.

Back-and-forth dialogue was referred to as *cross-talk* and two comics together on stage became known as a *double*.

Weber & Fields, although certainly not the first comedy duo, became the most accomplished and influential team of their generation. Their success paved the way for the next 130+ years of onstage doubles like Gallagher & Sheen, Williams & Walker, Smith & Dale, Olsen & Johnson, Wheeler & Woolsey, Butterbeans & Susie, Block & Sully, Clark & McCollough, Miller & Lyles, Laurel & Hardy, Burns & Allen, Abbott & Costello, Martin & Lewis, Allen & Rossi, Wayne & Shuster, Nichols & May, Rowan & Martin, Skiles & Henderson, the Smothers Brothers, Stiller & Meara, Burns & Schreiber, Tim & Tom, Cheech &

Chong, the Funny Boys, Mack & Jamie, the Sklar Brothers, and the Lucas Brothers.

Although comedy teams were all the rage in vaudeville, the solo monologist was starting to gain real traction at this time. These performers still used ethnic and racial stereotypes to get laughs but they figured out a way to make it work without using a partner. In a sense, the audience became their partner.

Acts like John T. Kelly (Irish), Jack Pearl (German), Cliff Gordon (German), Lou Holtz (Hebrew), and Joe Welch (Hebrew) are representative of hundreds of monologists that later became categorized as "dialect comedians."

But a quiet comedy revolution was underway in vaudeville as more and more comedians decided to completely shed the old-school stereotypes – and just speak as themselves. One of the earliest practitioners of this style was Charlie Case, a small-time, blackface comic. Case would perform his relaxed, first-person monologues sitting in a chair while casually playing with a string.

Monologists Julius Tannen, Stuart Barnes, James Thornton, George Fuller Golden, and Frank Fay also adapted this new style of comedy. They were just regular fellows who would stroll out onto a vaudeville stage, tell some jokes or stories, maybe do a song, and leave. That was their act.

Frank Fay, in particular, is largely credited with creating the modern stand-up aesthetic: well-dressed, confident, glib, and acerbic. Fay got booked to emcee at the most prestigious theater of the vaudeville era, the Palace (in NYC). He wasn't the first monologist to emcee but he maximized his opportunity. Creatively ad-libbing between each act, Fay added a new level to the vaudeville experience. Instead of just nine unrelated performances, he was able to comedically tie the whole evening together. Audiences ate it up and he was held over at the Palace for an unprecedented twelve weeks.

Fay and the other monologists of vaudeville, performing comedy in this new way, directly influenced and inspired the next generation of young comedians - among them were Jack Benny, Milton Berle, and Bob Hope. When we discuss vaudeville, we are referring to a predominately white institution. Black variety performers were relegated to minstrel shows, medicine shows, tent shows, carnivals, roadhouses, and the circus. Bert Williams and his partner George Walker were among the few black performers who were allowed to cross over and perform in mainstream vaudeville.

But by the 1920s, there was a thriving concurrent black vaudeville circuit called the Theater Owners Bookers Association (TOBA). When you worked this chain, it was called doing "Toby" time.

Many successful screen and stage comedians like Mantan Moreland, Eddie Anderson, Dusty Fletcher, Tim Moore, Eddie Green, Lincoln Perry (aka Stepin Fetchit), and Dewey "Pigmeat" Markham all performed on this "separate but equal" theater chain.

One young sketch performer, dancer, and singer whose comedic talents were first discovered on the TOBA circuit, and would later become an American stand-up icon, was Jackie Mabley.

Vaudeville wasn't the only game in town for comics looking for experience and exposure. There were also revues and burlesque.

REVUES presented dancers, chorus girls, original songs, comedy sketches, and monologues performed by a permanent cast. The most popular and prestigious revue of this era was the *Ziegfeld Follies*. But the format spawned many competing shows such as Earl Carroll's *Vanities*, George White's *Scandals*, *The Passing Show, Artists and Models*, and the *Greenwich Village Follies*.

These revues provided great opportunity and income for comedy headliners, many of whom were poached from vaudeville. The ability to perform "in one" remained a valuable commodity. For example, in *The Passing Show of 1922*, comedian Fred Allen was called on to present three separate monologues during the show, to accommodate multiple scenery changes behind the curtain.

Comics like W.C. Fields, Frank Fay, Ed Wynn, Jack Benny, Bert Williams, Willie and Eugene Howard, Doc Rockwell, and Lou Holtz were all showcased in these revues.

Men dominated live comedy at this time, but early 20th century women were beginning to break through. Most used music as a trojan horse to showcase their comedic talents. Fanny Brice, Ray Cox, Nan Halperin, Beatrice Lilly, Mae West, and Sophie Tucker all augmented their comedy routines with rousing musical numbers.

One of the most successful, and now largely forgotten, performer who starred in both vaudeville *and* revues was the multi-talented Elsie Janis. She could act, write, sing, compose music, tell jokes, and do dozens of spot-on impressions (of headliners like Will Rogers, George M. Cohan, and Faye Templeton) to great acclaim.

During World War I, Janis became the first American performer to entertain U.S. combat troops, overseas, on the front lines. Janis was doing pop-up shows from the bed of a pickup truck near the battlefields of France, twenty years before the USO existed.

Ever since that conflict, comedians have followed Janis's lead and entertained U.S. soldiers, sailors, and airmen in war zones around the globe.

BURLESQUE rose to prominence alongside vaudeville. Where vaudeville performers had to abide by hyper strict speech codes, burlesque comics enjoyed a slightly wider latitude when it came to acceptable onstage language. Burlesque humor was a bit more rowdy and considered *low comedy*. It targeted working class audiences.

Burlesque theaters in New York City were first centered on the Lower East Side and in Harlem. The now *world-famous* Apollo Theater first opened in 1914 as Hurtig and Seamon's New Burlesque Theater – with a strict "whites only" policy.

The common denominator of all burlesque shows was scantily clad women parading around – what they used to call "cheesecake." Eventually some of these women began suggestively disrobing, teasing the audience. The Minsky Brothers, in NYC, put a huge sign outside their theaters: "Burlesque As You Like It – Not a Family Show." Burlesque was starting to brand itself as an adult alternative to *polite* vaudeville.

There were several burlesque circuits (called a "wheel") that fanned out across the country, but there were also theaters which housed *permanent stock companies* that would change up the show every week. This created an intense training ground for wannabe comics and a hierarchy where the alpha comedian in the troupe was christened the "top banana."

Burlesque was a specific school of comedy. It was more sketch-based and the comics had a look: baggy pants, loud ties, and hats (think Fozzie Bear). They all learned how to use powder puffs, slapsticks, and seltzer bottles to elicit laughs. They were taught physical "business" like mugging, eye rolling, double takes, spit takes, skulling, and pratfalls.

Every burlesque comic worth his salt knew dozens of stock

comedy sketches with names like "Floogle Street," "Niagara Falls," "Crazy House," or "Pay the Two Dollars."

Comedians like Pinky Lee, Red Buttons, Burt Lahr, Red Skelton, Phil Silvers, Joey Faye, Rags Ragland, Zero Mostel, B.S. Pully, Jimmy Savo, Abbott & Costello, Morey Amsterdam, Benny Rubin, Irv Benson, and Pigmeat Markham all spent time in the school of burlesque.

One of the first major technical innovations that attracted the attention and talents of vaudeville era comedians was audio recordings. These new-fangled discs and cylinders could play back a routine over and over again. Comedy recordings became a popular sub-genre for the fledgling record industry.

The first vaudevillian to gain significant traction in this new medium was dialect comic Cal Stewart who, starting around 1897, began recording his original humorous stories as "The Yankee Comedian" and then more famously as "Uncle Josh."

Stewart's trademark was a hearty, repetitive (aka annoying) laugh that punctuated his folksy tales. Where books and newspaper columns were once crucial in helping Mark Twain and Artemus Ward sell tickets on the road, Stewart's live appearances were bolstered by his record sales.

Another comic monologist, Marshall P. Wilder, was there at the birth of the recording industry. According to *The New York Times*, Wilder became the first professional comedian to ever record a routine onto a disc. The event took place during a press demonstration of Thomas Edison's new "improved" phonograph on May 12, 1888. No known copy of Wilder's historic comedy recording exists.

But a later Wilder comedy record, this one from 1906, called

"Stories About the Baby," begins with an impressive ahead-of-his-time trope, *"Have you ever noticed..."*

Wilder was a trailblazing, disabled performer who used his sunny disposition, work ethic, and positive thinking to help transcend his physical limitations. A self-described "hunchbacked dwarf" he dreamed of becoming a comedy monologist and an actor. Performing at a time when such physical characteristics could land a wannabe entertainer into a circus sideshow tent – Wilder achieved his goals. He got his first break performing monologues in Chautauguas (traveling adult education exhibitions) before hitting the vaudeville circuit.

But the breakthrough comedy record of the era wasn't from "Uncle Josh" or the indomitable Marshall P. Wilder – it was Joe Hayman's, "Cohen on the Telephone." Recorded in 1913, this Hebrew-dialect recording presented one side of a frustrating phone call between a first-time telephone user and his landlord. It was a runaway success and became the first comedy record to sell a million copies (according to Joseph Murrell's book, *Million Selling Records from the 1900s to the 1980s).*

Besides the enormous commercial success of the recording, "Cohen on the Telephone" is historically noteworthy for a couple other reasons.

1. It popularized the comedic technique of reacting to an unheard partner – basically creating a one-person comedy team. This device was used by other vaudeville era comics like George Jessel and then, nearly fifty years later, by comedy album breakout stars Shelley Berman and Bob Newhart. The phone technique is still used by comedians today.

2. "Cohen on the Telephone" was so successful that other performers of the day (like Barney Bernard, George Thompson, and Julius Tannen) recorded

their own versions of the *exact same routine.*
Apparently, it was okay back then to release a cover
version of a comedy bit.

So, how did it all end for vaudeville? It wasn't just one thing.
Vaudeville was choked out by multiple forces.

- The enormous popularity of motion pictures.
- The stock market crash of October 1929.
- And the rise of a new, free, national mass medium
  that would revolutionize entertainment and create
  millionaires out of several vaudeville monologists.

3

RADIO DAYS

All that the radio comedian has to show for his years of work and aggravation is the echo of forgotten laughter.

— FRED ALLEN

IN THE mid-to-late 1920s the American entertainment industry was becoming increasingly wired for sound. Many vaudeville and burlesque theaters added electronic speaker systems to accommodate the coming onslaught of talking pictures. Circuses, sports stadiums, and rodeos also began adding loudspeakers.

Performing onstage with a microphone became the latest addition to a comedian's skill set. This new technology wasn't just utilized for straight forward amplification. The stage mic, in the right hands, was a versatile tool that could create a conversational intimacy between performer and audience. Now comics could be *loud while speaking softly*. In both powerful and subtle ways, stage mics would impact how stand-up comedy was performed (in much the same way that electronic amplification transformed popular singing styles).

American citizens were also wiring up their own homes with radio consoles. Radio began as a localized, unregulated, amateur, do-it-yourself invention that was soon swallowed up by big business interests that merged talent, broadcasting facilities, radio manufacturing, and advertising savvy. These corporations connected local, independent radio stations and transformed them into large, powerful *networks*.

On Monday evening, November 15, 1926, NBC began broadcasting and has not stopped since.

The program on NBC's initial broadcast featured the stars of the Metropolitan opera, the New York Symphony Orchestra, pop singers, dance bands, plus comedians Weber & Fields, and Will Rogers. The live, four-and-one-half hour program originated from the Waldorf-Astoria Hotel, just several blocks away from where NBC currently broadcasts its late-night variety show *Saturday Night Live*.

CBS joined the fray on January 18, 1929.

It's hard to imagine now just how stunning radio technology must have seemed at the time. Invisible, silent waves floating through the air, able to pass through physical barriers, and then magically transform into audible entertainment "programs." For the first time in human history, people across thousands of miles could all hear the same voices – at the same time.

The immense power of radio comedy was quickly demonstrated when, out of Chicago, two entertainers wrote and acted in a program that centered on black dialect characters named Amos and Andy. When NBC began broadcasting episodes across its expanding network, it ignited a national sensation. Even movie theaters would pump in the newest, daily, 15-minute episode of *Amos 'n' Andy*, before running their films.

The show bolstered the sale of radio consoles, increased the reach and power of networks, and attracted a slew of companies eager to advertise on this new medium. *Amos 'n' Andy* (sponsored by Pepsodent toothpaste) was the radio industry's proof of concept.

The program lasted for 32 seasons.

Veteran vaudeville comedian Ed Wynn was an early adaptor of radio. For decades he had cultivated a dithering, giggly comic persona that he called "The Perfect Fool." In 1932, Texaco developed a new, higher-grade gasoline that met the octane requirement for emergency vehicles, like fire engines. They branded the gas Fire-Chief.

To raise consumer awareness of its new product, Texaco decided to sponsor Ed Wynn's new Tuesday night radio show. Soon the "The Perfect Fool" was now nationally known as the "The Fire Chief," complete with red fireman's hat.

Wynn wasn't complaining, his salary was a whopping $5,000 a week at a time when millions of Americans were unemployed or struggling to eke out a living during the Great Depression.

And that, in a nutshell, was radio. Audiences received free entertainment, delivered directly into their living rooms. And the sponsor got car owners to consider "quick-starting Fire-Chief gasoline" when they pulled into a Texaco filing station.

It was a Madison Avenue dream; the traveling salesman was now inside your home.

Ed Wynn battled singer/comedian Eddie Cantor (sponsored by Chase and Sanborn Coffee) for comic supremacy in network radio's earliest days. Cantor eventually won the ratings war, but broadcast historians are still divided on whether it was Wynn's or Cantor's show that first incorporated the reaction of an audience. In early radio, quiet studios were crucial for engineers to broadcast a pristine signal. But comedians wouldn't have it, they fed off live audience interaction. Sound engineers would just have to learn to adapt.

Eddie Cantor was a force of peppy energy: he conquered vaudeville, the Ziegfeld Follies, musical-comedies, films, and audio recordings. He introduced several hit songs including "If You Knew Susie," and the double-entendre showstopper, "Makin' Whoopee." Cantor's various radio shows ran for 18 seasons.

Cantor began his show biz ascent when he was just sixteen,

winning an amateur night competition at Miner's Bowery Theatre in New York City. Miner's Theatre is credited with inventing the amateur night concept back in the 1880s, a crowd favorite that was later adopted by hundreds of vaudeville houses and clubs across the land. (The Apollo Theater's legendary amateur night began in 1934).

Broadcast networks joined the talent competition bonanza starting with NBC's *Original Amateur Hour* in 1934, hosted first by Major Bowes and then Ted Mack. Subsequent talent competition shows include *Arthur Godfrey's Talent Scouts, Great American Laugh Off, America's Funniest Comedian, Star Search, Last Comic Standing,* and *America's Got Talent.*

Comedians have been using talent competitions to help kick-start their careers for over 130 years now. Besides Eddie Cantor, the list includes Fred Allen, Redd Foxx, Jack Carter, Lenny Bruce, John Byner, Paul Rodriguez, Eddie Murphy, Dana Carvey, Rosie O'Donnell, Doug Stanhope, Sinbad, Mitch Hedberg, Amy Schumer, Gary Gulman, and Fortune Feimster.

During radio's golden era there were no talk show hosts like Jimmy Fallon or Conan O'Brien who booked rising young comedians. But radio did have *two* prime time variety shows that played a significant role in introducing listeners to the next generation of comics.

Most notably, pop singer Rudy Vallee (sponsored by Fleischmann's Yeast) gave early "coast-to-coast" exposure to aspiring comedy acts like Red Skelton, George Burns & Gracie Allen, Joe Penner, Edgar Bergen & Charlie McCarthy, Milton Berle, Bob Burns, Bob Hope, Al Bernie, and Phil Silvers.

And singer Kate Smith gave comedians Henny Youngman, Jackie Gleason, and Abbott & Costello a shot on her popular NBC show.

* Side note: Years later, in the mid-1960s, Rudy Vallee continued his tradition of presenting new talent. On his televi-

sion show, *On Broadway Tonight*, he gave both Richard Pryor and Rodney Dangerfield their first national TV exposure.

Radio presented a huge challenge for comedians... material. Vaudeville comics could tour with the same act for years, honing it to can't-miss perfection. In fact, many variety performers, when they retired, would auction off their bulletproof acts. Or bequeath it to their children.

However radio was a different animal; the medium devoured comedy material at an astonishing rate. Vaudeville comics had used joke books, joke magazines, and specialty writers (like Al Boasberg) to help develop or shape their routines. But network radio demanded such a huge volume of new punchlines that the full-time, professional, comedy writer entered the marketplace. This is when and where the "writers' room" was created.

When Bob Hope finally got his own radio program, he invested a large portion of his salary hiring a crew of gag writers. They were expected to be on call 24/7. These writers were not just there for his NBC radio show, but *any time* Mr. Hope needed to be funny: personal appearances, charity events, writing his "memoir," military shows, planned ad-libs, award ceremonies, and even on-set movie punch up.

To Hope's credit, he never hid the fact that he had a *team* of writers feeding him lines. Instead, he embraced it. A dependence on writers became part of his comedy persona.

Hope, and his ace writing crew, focused a great deal of their time and attention on his program's opening monologue. Other radio comics, like Eddie Cantor, began their shows humorously bantering with their announcer or band leader, allowing listeners to ease into the meat of the show.

Hope wasn't having that. He opened his radio show with

guns a-blazing. Hope, with his potent combination of ease and confidence, served up stand-up monologues consisting of on-the-mark topical jokes along with a dash of self-deprecating one-liners. It was fast and snappy.

Will Rogers first demonstrated the inherent comedic juice of "topical humor" and then Bob Hope refined and supercharged it.

Fred Allen was a different kind of radio comic, to put it mildly. Looking back, it's kind of miraculous that his show became one of the most popular in radio history. Allen was a brilliant, dour, acerbic, cynical, and satirical comedian who often seemed to despise the very industry that made him a household name.

Allen embraced writing his radio show as much as performing it. And although he did utilize a writers' room, Allen was the primary creative force. That meant he meticulously micro-managed 39 original scripts every year. The grind weighed on him; he aged rapidly, and his sky-high blood pressure forced him to take a long medical hiatus in the middle of his 17-season run.

Blessed with a wildly creative mind, Allen was one of the few comedians of that era who wrote all of his own material. From his earliest days, struggling in vaudeville as a juggler, he was searching for innovative ways to perform. He had an epiphany when he shared the bill with an act named Griff who, in clown makeup, made bubbles and did ventriloquism. Allen realized it was all just a giant misdirect, and that the essence of Griff's act wasn't about bubble making, it was just a vehicle for his verbal comedy.

Soon Allen was jotting down random notes and comedic ideas into his personal notebook – which he always carried. He started speaking onstage more and billed himself as "the world's worst juggler." His act became *making fun of his own act.* The audiences who got it, loved it. It was all very meta, and way ahead of its time. Over 50 years later, Steve Martin, Albert Brooks, and David Letterman utilized a similar comedic approach.

———

Jack Benny, whose radio popularity stands above all the others, was a pitch perfect comic for this new electronic-age medium. His unhurried, nonchalant delivery made for wonderfully easy listening.

Benny and his writing staff realized that building a specific comedic persona was the best strategy to maintain their show's potency year after year. So "Jack Benny" was given two primary character weaknesses to hang jokes on: vanity and stinginess. For decades he claimed to be just 39-years-old.

Like the sitcom *Seinfeld*, Benny surrounded himself with a superb supporting cast which allowed him to react. He was essentially the straight man in the middle of a comedic storm. And react he did. Benny was blessed with impeccable timing.

Benny didn't slave over scripts like Fred Allen; he hired talented writers and let them do their thing. But he did have an innate talent that he often said was a key to his supremacy on radio – the ability to edit. He seemed to just know what would – and wouldn't – work. He often tweaked the scripts right up to showtime.

And, in a lucky stroke of marketing genius, Jack Benny and Fred Allen accidentally created a "feud" between the two programs. When they realized how popular their weekly on-air insults were, it proved a ratings bonanza for both shows.

The Jack Benny Show ran for 23 years.

Not all radio stations were part of the powerful national networks. Local and regional stations had their own programming and developed their own talent pool. One of the most influential stations was WSM in Nashville, which helped popularize country music and was instrumental in making the city of Nashville a music recording mecca.

On November 30, 1940, comic monologist Minnie Pearl made her debut on *The Grand Ole Opry*, WSM's flagship radio program. She was an immediate hit, and Minnie spent the next fifty years performing her homespun comedy on radio, television, and in live performances.

The same year Minnie Pearl started on radio in Nashville, a local station in New York City (WOR) gave a brilliant, improvisational monologist named Henry Morgan a daily, fifteen-minute program. The audacious Morgan, often working without a script, gained a dedicated cult following (including future stand-ups George Carlin and Mort Sahl). But, ultimately, he sabotaged any chance of mainstream success because he couldn't resist viciously lampooning his sponsors.

In the 1940s, three future-hosts of NBC's *Tonight Show* – Steve Allen, Jack Paar, and Johnny Carson – all cut their teeth doing comedy bits on local radio. As did the wildly innovative Ernie Kovacs, who also briefly hosted *The Tonight Show*. And, beginning in 1946, local Boston station WHDH gave listeners the wonderfully inventive comedy team of Bob & Ray.

But by the early 1950s there was no stopping the new kid on the block... television. The next generation of comics were taking over and the old network radio legends were forced to adapt or fade away.

As for radio, it became increasingly driven by music, news, sports, and talk. But, on a much smaller scale, scripted radio comedy never really ended. There was still a bit of breathing room for the likes of Stan Freberg, Jean Shepherd, the *National Lampoon Radio Hour,* Garrison Keillor, and, eventually, scripted podcasts.

4

NIGHTCLUBS, RESORTS, AND THEATERS

When I do an hour-and-a-half show, if I don't improvise 20 minutes worth of new material each night, I feel I've let myself down.

— BUDDY HACKETT

AS VAUDEVILLE died off, some comics just retired, others got real jobs, and many migrated over to nightclubs where a new way of doing comedy was being created.

The shows in these nightclubs were for adults. The clownish baggy-pants & loud-tie look was out, replaced by sharp suits and tuxedos. Smoking and drinking were expected and encouraged. And although there wasn't much profanity (yet), adult themed material, that could have gotten a comic banned from the Orpheum circuit, was more accepted and appreciated.

There was a variety aspect to a nightclub show. On very rare occasions more than one comedian would be on the bill. Typically, the lineup consisted of a singer or dance band, a specialty act, and the comic. And in the bigger rooms, full revues with chorus girls.

Some clubs were situated inside beautiful, ornate hotels while others hid out in the seedier sections of town.

Nightclub headliners like Joe E. Lewis, Sophie Tucker, Jimmy Durante, The Ritz Brothers, Milton Berle, and Danny Thomas battled for laughs over the din of booze and food service.

Many of these nightclubs grew out of the speakeasies, taverns, honky-tonks, and saloons that blossomed during the nearly thirteen years (1920-1933) when the manufacturing, transporting, and sale of alcohol was prohibited by a constitutional amendment.

When prohibition was lifted, America's nightclub era began in earnest, although it didn't peak until the 1940s. Most of these clubs were owned and run by ex-bootleggers and organized crime syndicates. More than a few doubled as fronts for illegal gambling and/or prostitution.

The most legendary nightclubs of this era featured "exotic" foreign sounding names that contrasted sharply with their mobster/hoodlum underpinnings: Chez Paree, Copacabana, Latin Quarter, El Morocco, Café Zanzibar, Ciro's, La Martinique, Macambo, etc., etc., etc.

Night life was sweeping through America's big cities. Respectable men and women now openly drank and socialized alongside film stars, show girls, pro athletes, gangsters, politicians, press agents, and newspaper columnists. At New York's Copacabana, shows were scheduled at 8pm, midnight, and 2am. Atlantic City's 500 Club offered a similar schedule... *plus* a 4am performance.

Some clubs had a full stage while others just used the dance floor as the performance area. It was called a floor show. This created close-up comedy with audiences often seated just inches from the performer. In this environment, a comic with a knack for improvisation and ad-libbing could sometimes win over an indifferent crowd, creating an entire show based on audience interaction.

Comedians like Jack Waldron, Jack E. Leonard, Don Rickles, Jack White, and Jackie Gleason built their acts around working the crowd. Leonard and Rickles, in particular, became legendary "insult comics" with lightning-fast improvs that gave their acts a heightened you-had-to-be-there juice.

Modern era *crowd work* comedians like Richard Belzer, Jimmy Brogan, Pudgy, Robin Harris, Paula Poundstone, Jeffrey Ross, Ian Bagg, Dave Attell, Judah Friedlander, Jimmy Pardo, Todd Barry, Lisa Lampanelli, Ben Gleib, Moshe Kasher, and Big Jay Oakerson have continued this nightclub tradition.

Racial segregation continued well into the nightclub era. Several of the most successful and famous rooms in Harlem, like The Cotton Club, had all-black entertainment that catered almost exclusively to a white clientele.

In 1923, comic/singer/dancer Jackie Mabley made a splash at the Harlem nightclub, Connie's Inn. Mabley, like most other female comedy pioneers of that era, used music to help present her comedy material. Through years of trial and error, she developed a comic persona of a naughty, truth-telling, man-hungry (always the younger ones) matron who dressed in a shabby, thrift store housecoat. She called her "Moms."

Moms Mabley became a trailblazing female stand-up who, later in life, gained a huge nationwide fanbase following the racial integration of nightclubs in the early 1960s. Unfortunately, the bulk of Mabley's comedy career was siloed in what became known as the *chitlin' circuit* – a collection of clubs and theaters that featured entertainment for-and-by African Americans. Harlem's Apollo Theater became the crown jewel of this circuit.

The circuit included old TOBA theaters like the Regal in Chicago, the Howard in D.C., the Royal in Baltimore, and the Standard in Philly. This breeding ground helped develop the next generation of stand-ups like Timmie Rogers, Redd Foxx, Slappy White, and Nipsey Russell.

One of the rare integrated nightclubs pre-1960 was Café Society in Greenwich Village. Jack Gilford was their regular emcee and, in the late 1930s, his creative, alt-style act included esoteric impressions of pea soup boiling or a flickering florescent light. Gilford was part of a trend that saw many young comics get their stage legs as a regular "house emcee."

- "Jumpin'" Jackie Gleason, had a three-year run as the house emcee (and bouncer) at the Miami Club in Newark, New Jersey.
- Nipsey Russell clocked in a six-year emcee stint at the Club Baby Grand on 125th street, where he was known as "Harlem's Son of Fun."
- Jack White was part owner and the regular emcee at Club 18. The midtown Manhattan nightclub became legendary for "roasting" the customers.
- Comedian Billy Gray was the resident emcee for over a decade at his own Los Angeles nightclub, Billy Gray's Band Box on Fairfax Avenue.

Comics coming up in the 1930s found stage time opportunities in some rather grim circumstances. One particularly cruel gig was emceeing walkathons. This was the idea: financially desperate young couples would walk around in a large circle day after day, and the objective was to... not collapse. The last couple standing would win a substantial cash prize. This phenomenon was chronicled in the 1969 film, *They Shoot Horses, Don't They?*

Walkathons were extremely popular depression-era competitions that could last months (there were rest periods). Local radio stations broadcast live updates. Spectators, for just pennies a day, could keep returning and cheer on their favorite couple. To keep the "energy going" promotors hired gift-of-gab come-

dians like Harry Jarkey, Lord Buckley, and Red Skelton to improvise the heartbreaking, play-by-play action.

———————

In New York City, the aspiring young comics of this era had their
own hangout in midtown Manhattan: Hanson's Drugstore. It
was located on the ground floor of an office building at 1650
Broadway. Dozens of ambitious comics like Buddy Hackett, Jack
Roy (later rebranded as Rodney Dangerfield), Adam Keefe, Will
Jordan, Don Sherman, Lenny Bruce, Jackie Miles, kibitzed,
riffed, and schmoozed the hours away.

Low-rung "Hanson comics" dreamed of one day obtaining
high paying gigs at one of the many plush nightclubs that were
within walking distance of their comedy clubhouse: the Copa,
the Latin Quarter, and Nicky Blair's Carnival to name a few.
Midtown was also home to smaller rooms like Club 18, Leon and
Eddies, Playgoers Club, and the China Doll.

Plus, Broadway and 7th Avenue were adorned with spectac-
ular movie palaces: the Roxy, the Strand, the Paramount, the
Capital, Loew's State, and (over on 6th Avenue) Radio City
Music Hall.

At the time, every one of these giant movie cathedrals
booked comedians as part of variety shows that were presented
prior to the feature films. These mega-theaters were called
presentation houses. *Billboard* magazine categorized them as
Vaudefilm.

There were usually five or six shows-a-day (up to eight on
weekends) in presentation houses. The hours were long, but the
pay could be spectacular. At his peak, Milton Berle pulled down
an astonishing $35,000 a week headlining the 6,000-seat Roxy.

Alan King, Jerry Lester, Jack Carter, Henny Youngman, Jack
E. Leonard, Jan Murray, and Phil Foster all worked these presen-

tation houses. At the Capitol Theater Bob Hope first did on-stage schtick with his future film partner, Bing Crosby. And Jerry Lewis was an usher at Loew's State years before he and Dean Martin made their traffic-stopping, Beatlemania-esque debut at the Paramount.

The nightclub comic's world was primarily a boys' club until around 1945, when Jean Carroll burst onto the scene. Carroll, who was part of a double act (with her husband), decided to try her luck as a *single*. She dressed elegantly and began cracking sharp jokes about her modern life as a wife, mother, and career woman.

Turns out Carroll was a natural stand-up. She quickly worked her way up to headlining status in presentation houses, major nightclubs, resorts, and eventually television. Carroll is one of stand-up's trailblazers, now nearly forgotten, who inspired many young entertainers, most notably Lily Tomlin.

Hanson's Drugstore was also directly below the offices of multiple theatrical agents who were toiling on the upper floors of 1650 Broadway. It was especially convenient for comics hustling for bookings or new representation. But one specific agency was especially critical to the livelihood of this generation of comics: it was called Charles Rapp Enterprises, but was known simply as the *Rapp office*. Rapp was the primary booker for more than 100 entertainment venues in the Catskills.

Also known as the Borscht Belt, the Catskill Mountains were about 90 miles outside of NYC and had hundreds of hotels – ranging from large resorts, to small bungalow colonies. It was a popular summer destination for Greek, Polish, Italian, and Irish working class families. But the region became most noted for serving a Jewish clientele.

Many of the hotels were strictly kosher (milk and dairy at breakfast and lunch, meat for dinner). At the resorts, families paid a flat fee for their room, three meals a day – *and* athletic activities – *and* social activities – *and* entertainment. It was a good deal plus a nice escape from the city's stifling summer heat.

The Catskills provided seasonal employment to scores of young comics of the nightclub era. They called it "working the mountains." And the Rapp office was their golden ticket.

Almost every resort hired social directors – aka *tummlers* (Yiddish for "creator of exciting tumult"). They were high-energy funny guys who were expected to creatively entertain the guests 24/7, often performing "crazy" stunts like walking into the swimming pool fully clothed. They also helped facilitate social activities like bingo, tennis lessons, square dancing, or Simon Says.

The money wasn't great, but it did provide the most valuable commodity for young comics: stage time.

Danny Kaye was the first *mountain* entertainer (Kaye was actually discovered in the nearby Pocono Mountains of Pennsylvania) to go from tummler to nightclubs to Broadway and then films. Kaye's movies, which showcased his remarkable verbal dexterity, were a major inspiration for a young George Carlin.

Scores of comics like Buddy Hackett, Mel Brooks, Alan King, Jackie Mason, Jerry Lewis, Joey Adams, and Henny Youngman honed their stage personas in the Catskills.

Every single comic mentioned in the preceding paragraph was Jewish. And most continued the vaudeville tradition of de-Jewing their old world names. For example, Benjamin Kubelsky became Jack Benny. Cultural assimilation was the goal for Jewish comedians in the first half of the 20th century.

- Mendel Berlinger – Milton Berle
- Leonard Hacker – Buddy Hackett
- Aaron Chiwat – Red Buttons
- Celine Zeigman – Jean Carroll
- Melvin Kaminsky – Mel Brooks
- Irwin Kniberg – Alan King

- Jerome Levitch – Jerry Lewis
- Yakov Mosher Maza – Jackie Mason
- David Kaminsky – Danny Kaye
- Joseph Gottlieb – Joey Bishop
- Sheldon Greenfield – Shecky Greene
- Leonard Schneider – Lenny Bruce

In the end, though, despite their efforts to obscure their religious heritage: Buddy, Milton, Lenny, Mel, Shecky, and Joey didn't sound particularly WASPy.

The Catskill venues weren't the only seasonal employment available for the nightclub comics of that era. For a few months a year, from roughly January through March, Miami came alive with club activity. In-demand comics booked their "summer" in the mountains, and their "winter" in Miami Beach.

Miami's peak activity coincided with the thoroughbred racing season at Hialeah Park. Legalized pari-mutuel betting on horses, greyhounds, and jai alai helped ignite a massive south Florida construction boom that continued into the 2000s. Modern state-of-the-art hotels like The Fontainebleau, The Eden Roc, and The Americana rose up from repurposed swamp land.

It was a wild, unregulated scene. Large and small mob-run nightclubs were sprinkled all over town: The Beachcomber, Latin Quarter, Murray Franklin's, Ciro's, Mother Kelly's, The Paddock Bar, The Clover Club, The Five O'Clock Club, and Place Pigalle all provided stages for the next generation of upstart comics.

Boozed up "snowbirds" enjoyed comedians like Rip Taylor, B.S. Pully, Joe E. Ross, Sammy Shore, Jackie Miles, Shecky Greene, Myron Cohen, Don Rickles, Gene Baylos, and Jan Murray.

Two comic/singers, Belle Barth and Pearl Williams, were

also part of the Miami scene. Inspired by the success of night-club legend Sophie Tucker and her double-entendre stage patter, they both pushed the boundaries of sexual innuendo a couple steps further. Although never graphically obscene, Barth and Williams fell into the *naughty* category. Years later, recordings of their live shows would be part of the adult "party record" craze.

But in the late 1940s, 2,500 miles away from balmy Miami Beach, construction began on a new resort location in the middle of the desert. The hotel casinos that would spring up would become the nightclub comic's dream destination: Las Vegas, Nevada. The self-proclaimed, "Entertainment Capital of The World."

The Catskills and Miami Beach were primarily seasonal destinations, but Las Vegas was a year-round operation. And although the desert had no scenic mountain lakes or ocean beaches close by, Vegas did provide roulette, poker, blackjack, Keno, slot machines, topless showgirls, and prostitution. All legal. And air-conditioned.

The huge Vegas showrooms became the newest and most prestigious booking for the Copa generation of comics. Because revenue was generated by the nightly casino "drop," as opposed to ticket sales, comedian's salaries jumped to new heights. Comedian Red Buttons once commented that after a four week run in Vegas, a comic could buy a third world country.

And the Vegas comedy explosion wasn't exclusively in the huge, lush showrooms. The small lounges became laboratories for wild, experimental late-night comedy. Two comics in particular, Shecky Greene (at the Riviera) and Don Rickles (at the Sahara) showcased their lightning-fast improvisation skills. Working the lounge at The Sahara, Rickles was contracted to perform three shows a night: midnight, 2:30am, and a 5:10am "breakfast show."

It was during the nightclub era that a new descriptor for comedians was born: stand-up. *Variety*, the show business trade magazine, first printed that term on June 23, 1948, in their review of vaudeville legend Lou Holtz's gig at the L.A. nightclub, Slapsy Maxie's.

It was a versatile descriptor. Bob Hope might sing a duet with Marilyn Maxwell, perform some bits with Jerry Colonna, and then do fifteen minutes of stand-up. It was something you do (verb), something you are (noun), and also a modifier (adjective).

The exact origin of the term remains in dispute among comedy historians. Some are convinced that it was created by comedy bookers, agents, and entertainment writers as a short-hand description of a specific kind of act: a comedian who didn't use props, or music charts, or special lighting cues... it was just jokes.

Another version of stand-up's etymology comes from veteran comedian Dick Curtis, as quoted in Kliph Nesteroff's essential book, *The Comedians*. Curtis believed it was all something that the mafia created, "The Outfit used to manage fighters. A stand-up fighter is a guy that is a puncher. A stand-up guy was a guy who was tough and you could depend on. The Outfit managed fighters and they managed clubs that booked comics, so the term found its way into the lexicon of nightclubs. A guy who just stood there and punched jokes—joke, joke, joke—he was a stand-up comic."

When the term "stand-up" first appeared in the late 1940s; nightclubs, presentation houses, and the resorts had all but vanquished what was left of vaudeville and burlesque. But, at the time, no one could have imagined that this seemingly all-powerful entertainment ecosystem would soon be challenged by an unlikely comedy wave. This revolution, led by new comics getting laughs in new ways, would both delight and disgust audiences.

5

TV AND THE NEW WAVE

I can't think of anything more unsatisfying than trying to be intelligent in a nightclub. What's the point of talking politics and sociology to a bunch of drunks?

— JACKIE GLEASON

IN JUNE of 1948, the same month that *Variety* first used the term "stand-up," two historic television shows debuted just days part.

NBC's *Texaco Star Theater* went on the air June 8th, and then CBS's *The Ed Sullivan Show* (originally called *Toast of the Town*) began its run on June 20th. At the time, few would have guessed that Sullivan would have the greater comedic impact.

The *Texaco Star Theater* was television's Big Bang moment. It was hosted by 40-year-old Milton Berle – a holdover from the last days of vaudeville who was the current king of nightclub comics. In 1946, Berle was making $10,000 a week at a NY supper club called Nicky Blair's Carnival.

When the brash, high-energy Berle became the permanent host of Texaco, viewers couldn't get enough. Watching the outrageous Berle on Tuesday night became television's first must-see event. The show was broadcast live from a converted radio studio (6B) inside the RCA Building,

Berle's ratings were absurd: he often had over 80 percent of all viewers watching his show. It was a wild social happening, and soon the newly crowned "Mr. Television" graced the cover of *Newsweek* and *Time* in the same week. Network TV had finally arrived in America, and its first megastar was a comedian. Milton Berle became an instant legend and a role model for young comics dreaming of the big time. After his TV tapings and local club dates, Berle would hold court at NY's Lindy's restaurant and all the working comedians would congregate for late-night insults, sandwiches, soup, and cheesecake. (This tradition of an after-show "hang" was echoed at eateries like Wolfie's in Miami Beach, Red Apple Rest outside the Catskills, the Green Kitchen near Catch A Rising Star, the Olive Tree above the Comedy Cellar, and Canter's or Ben Frank's/Mel's in L.A.)

Although Berle's Texaco show was red hot in 1948, the outlook was not as rosy over at CBS. Its Sunday evening variety program was hosted by a painfully awkward New York gossip columnist named Ed Sullivan. The premiere was uneventful except for marking the television debut of the comedy team of Dean Martin and Jerry Lewis. The sponsor wanted to replace Sullivan as soon as possible. He was awkward, wooden, and not the least bit telegenic.

However, the program's eclectic, vaudeville-inspired, family-friendly lineup began gaining loyal viewers and, by 1955, the Sullivan show was a ratings juggernaut. Over 40 million people tuned in each week. And the *Texaco Star Theater*, along with every other primetime variety show since, never came close to matching Sullivan's popularity and longevity. The show ran from 1948 until 1971.

Ed Sullivan is now best remembered for booking legendary music acts, notably Elvis Presley in 1956 and the Beatles in 1964, but almost every broadcast featured at least one stand-up, comedy team, impressionist, or ventriloquist performing their six or seven minute routine (in the 1950s the comics sometimes did up to ten minutes). America got to *see*, for the first time, comedians do their stand-up routines on television.

Over the show's 23-year run, Sullivan showcased hundreds of comedy acts, primarily from the nightclub/resort generation. Jack Carter, Myron Cohen, Alan King, and Jean Carroll were the stand-ups with the most appearances over the life of the show.

Scoring on Sullivan was often a career-making moment. After an impressive performance a comic could book dates at bigger nightclubs or even open for singers in Vegas. Jan Murray, Jackie Mason, Totie Fields, Will Jordan, Norm Crosby, George Kirby, and Jack E. Leonard were among hundreds of comics who got priceless TV exposure on Sullivan. Prior to their "shot" many had been struggling no-names, hanging out at Hanson's, hoping for a break.

In every era, starting with vaudeville, comedians lusted after a single, much desired, prestige booking. These dream opportunities provided top-shelf exposure, and the stamp of legitimacy. That dream booking changed through the generations: *The Ziegfeld Follies*, the Palace, the Copacabana, *The Ed Sullivan Show* – and then later *The Tonight Show*, HBO, and Netflix.

———

As nightclubs, Vegas, the Catskills, resorts, and presentation houses dominated the comedy landscape, there was a concurrent network of smaller, more intimate clubs that helped cultivate a new wave of stand-ups. These venues usually featured jazz or folk music. One such room was San Francisco's hungry i.

There was nothing plush or swank or schmantzy about the hungry i. It was located in a basement and the acts performed in front of an exposed brick wall. It was as if the ornate facade of show business had been sandblasted away. The audiences were smart and attentive. Hecklers were shown the door. The room, to quote the vernacular of the day, was "hip."

It was in this progressive environment, at the hungry i, that a local comedian named Mort Sahl began to find his style. No joke-jokes. No rim shots. And no sharp suits or tuxedos for Sahl. Partially inspired by the conversational tone of a radio comic named Herb Shriner – Sahl didn't look, or sound, like a confident nightclub comedian. He dressed like a grad student: V-neck sweater and open collared shirt. His delivery was halting, choppy, and loose. He often brought a rolled up newspaper onstage with him, not to slap someone with, but to indicate what he might be talking about today. It was 1953 and America had just elected its first Republican president in twenty years.

Sahl presented stand-up in a new way: conversational, literate, and satirical. With a boost from several San Francisco newspaper columnists, Sahl gained a following rather quickly. It seemed that more than just west coast "intellectuals" or "bohemians" were thirsty for this new kind of comedy.

Touring with Dave Brubeck's jazz combo, Sahl did shows at several colleges and universities. This opened a new booking opportunity for generations of comedians.

Sahl's reputation grew and he was soon playing nightclubs, similar to the hungry i, that were part of an emerging jazz and comedy aesthetic. Performing at two of these clubs, Mister Kelly's in Chicago and the Blue Angel in New York City, Sahl inspired two future comedy stars to give stand-up a try. One was an improv performer named Shelley Berman, and the other was a young comedy writer: Woody Allen.

In 1958, the jazz label Verve recorded Sahl's act at the hungry i. That album, *The Future Lies Ahead*, was not the first long-playing live comedy album released – Redd Foxx had beat him to the punch – but it was certainly a cultural breakthrough.

And it helped usher in the American comedy record boom.

Mort Sahl became the Moses of this new comedy movement. He was profiled in *The New Yorker* and *Playboy* and even graced the cover of *Time* magazine. That article drew comparisons to Mark Twain, Artemus Ward, and Will Rogers.

Next up in the late-50s comedy record boom was Shelley Berman, a Chicago-based improv performer who turned to stand-up. Berman was a member of The Compass Players, the legendary improv troupe that basically *started* improv in America.

At the Compass, Berman began developing long-form routines that utilized the comedic technique of reacting to a voice on the other end of a phone call, echoing Joe Hayman's classic "Cohen on the Telephone" record from 1913. But after seeing Mort Sahl at Mister Kelly's, Berman thought that, perhaps, his telephone monologues could be repurposed for the clubs. So, he tried his luck as a single.

Berman presented routines while sitting on a bar stool, which caused some entertainment writers to categorize him as a "sit-down" comedian. His debut comedy album, *Inside Shelley Berman* (Verve, 1959), also recorded at the hungry i, was an instant hit – easily outselling Sahl's.

The record became the industry's first gold comedy album (500,000+ copies) and Berman went on to win the Grammy Award for Best Comedy Performance – Spoken. He was the first stand-up to win in that category. And then, on March 12, 1960, Shelley Berman became the first modern stand-up to headline NYC's Carnegie Hall. (Will Rogers played Carnegie back in 1926.) It was heady stuff for a newbie.

But then along came Bob Newhart.

Newhart released what is, arguably, the most unlikely

comedy album ever recorded: *The Button-Down Mind of Bob Newhart* (Warner Bros., 1960). The cuts on the album were culled from Newhart's *very first* nightclub gig. The record became a phenomenon and easily eclipsed the sales of both Sahl and Berman, staying at number one on the pop charts for fourteen weeks (not consecutively). It sold well over a million copies.

At the Grammy Awards, Newhart had a night for the ages. He won three awards: Best New Artist, Best Comedy Performance – Spoken, and Album of the Year (besting singers like Harry Belafonte, Frank Sinatra, and Nat King Cole).

Newhart made another bit of history when, on January 5, 1961, he filmed the very first stand-up special. Telemeter, an experimental pay TV company in Canada, produced the event. It was broadcast live and then replayed several times.

Bob Newhart's long-forgotten 70-minute telecast predates HBO's stand-up specials by nearly fifteen years.

Other influential new wave comics of the era – Lenny Bruce, Dick Gregory, Nichols and May, and Jonathan Winters – joined the comedy record parade.

The title of Lenny's first all stand-up album, *The Sick Humor of Lenny Bruce* (Fantasy Records, 1959), was his enthusiastic embrace of the critically dismissive "sick comic" label that came his way.

On July 13, 1959, *Time* magazine published a bizarre take-down of most of the crop of new wave comics. Entitled "The Sickniks," the article lumped a diverse crew of performers together: Jonathan Winters, Lenny Bruce, Shelley Berman, Tom Lehrer, Don Adams, and, most curiously, the team of Mike Nichols and Elaine May. But the majority of the article's ire was directed at Lenny. This was two years before he first got arrested for cursing onstage.

Lenny was gaining a reputation for using comedy to shine a light on the underbelly and hypocrisy of mid 20th-century American culture. Lenny leaned into previously taboo premises like drug use, interracial sex, the Holocaust, assassination, amputees, homosexuality, body shame, matricide, rape, masturbation, and organized religion. These weren't the type of stand-up bits one would usually hear at mountain hotels like The Concord or Grossinger's.

LP (long-playing) comedy albums were the forefathers of today's comedy specials. These records, for the first time ever, allowed fans to hear and "feel" the room as comics worked adult nightclubs, jazz rooms, and theaters. It was a powerfully immersive experience.

These records also allowed comedy fans to listen anytime, multiple times, and even transcribe and break down a comedian's act. Collecting and dissecting these recordings spawned a new generation of comedy nerds.

Also thriving in the early 1960s was an underground market for adult themed "party records," a niche originating with Redd Foxx's 1956's release: *Laff of the Party*. In-the-know buyers would inquire if these albums were available "behind the counter." Foxx opened the floodgates to hundreds of acts, on specialty labels, whose material ranged from frisky (Woody Woodbury) to raunchy (Rudy Ray Moore) to explicit (LaWanda Page).

Among the most popular recordings were the "bawdy" albums featuring women like Belle Barth, Ruth Wallis, Pearl Williams, and Rusty Warren of *Knockers Up* fame.

Most of the established nightclub headliners were skeptical of the emerging comedy record boom. Why, they would ask, should they give away their act for $1.98 when they were pulling down $18,000 a week in Vegas? This created a generation gap, with new wave comics viewing comedy records as a valuable promotional tool and creative exercise – while the older comedians remained unconvinced.

This was also the era when the walls of comedic racial segregation were finally torn down, thanks to Chicago comic Dick Gregory. African American comics, as a rule, were not booked into white nightclubs or resorts like Vegas or the Catskills. They were relegated to the chitlin circuit. But, gradually, cracks in the walls developed. Dancer, singer, and comic Timmie Rogers played a few white nightclubs in the '40s and '50s as an opening act. Redd Foxx worked NY's jazz club Basin Street East in 1959, also as an opener. But on a cold January night in 1961, things changed forever.

The newly opened Playboy Club in Chicago took a chance on local comedian Dick Gregory. He walked onstage, in front of an all-white crowd, and performed smart, urbane material – primarily about race relations. The audience ate it up. He went over so well that he was rebooked immediately.

Gregory's successful headlining gig at the Playboy Club became a huge national news story. It was first reported in a glowing *Time* magazine article, followed by *Newsweek, The New York Times,* and *Esquire.* That press onslaught, along with a series of engaging appearances on Jack Paar's *Tonight Show,* catapulted his career to the top tier.

Fourteen years after the major leagues desegregated baseball, stand-up comedy had its own Jackie Robinson. In Gregory's wake, Slappy White, Redd Foxx, Moms Mabley, Nipsey Russell, and Timmie Rogers all began to finally obtain mainstream bookings in clubs, resorts, and on TV variety and talk shows.

Dick Gregory made six appearances on Jack Paar's *Tonight Show* in 1961. He first refused to appear unless he could also be interviewed after his set. People took notice. The impact of late-night television on a young comic's career was real.

Buddy Hackett, Joey Bishop, Nipsey Russell, Phyllis Diller, Orson Bean, Mort Sahl, the Smothers Brothers, Shelley Berman, along with dozens of other comedians – were also showcased by Paar.

Acts that were too avant-garde for *The Ed Sullivan Show*, like Jonathan Winters, could now find a broadcast outlet and build a fan base. Winters, whose improvisational genius inspired scores of comics, made over 65 appearances with Jack Paar.

Comedy was becoming more experimental and satirical. Topics, once off-limits, were now creeping into stand-up and onto late-night television. One example of this trend was a recurring Jack Paar guest, Oscar Levant. Although not a stand-up (he was a concert pianist), Levant comedically riffed about his own mental illness, prescription drug addiction, depression, and electric shock therapy sessions. This was the beginning of what became known as *confessional comedy*, where comedians found laughs in tragic, humiliating, dark, and shameful aspects of their personal lives.

In 1962, after hosting for five years, Jack Paar walked away from *The Tonight Show*. Johnny Carson, a young comic and game show host, took over. He would host for the next thirty years.

The new wave of comedians that emerged in the late 1950s, led by Mort Sahl, Dick Gregory, Jonathan Winters, and Lenny Bruce, pushed the evolution of stand-up comedy. Their humor was sometimes lost on boozed-up patrons in traditional night-clubs, but it landed nicely with a growing legion of appreciative comedy fans.

Around 1960, in downtown Manhattan, another comedic breeding ground would emerge. Borrowing the template of inti-mate jazz clubs, with their low ceilings and hip audiences, this

Greenwich Village scene would attract the next generation of young comics looking for a break.

Among them were five performers who would establish a new standard for comedic excellence: Bill Cosby, George Carlin, Joan Rivers, Woody Allen, and Richard Pryor.

6

COFFEEHOUSES, COMEDY CLUBS, AND CARSON

I had no big break. It was a combination of a lot of things: sixteen Ed Sullivan Shows, seventy times on the Tonight Show, forty-five Merv Griffin Shows...

— RODNEY DANGERFIELD

IN THE early 1960s Greenwich Village became the newest magnet for young comics looking to develop their acts and get on television. It was a scene: art galleries, small theaters, late-night bookstores, jazz clubs, chess games, dance studios, coffeehouses, restaurants, and an exploding musical scene called the "folk revival."

Every weekend the Village was packed with tourists, bohemians, intellectuals, students, and wannabe hipsters from Westchester, New Jersey, and Long Island. This lively environment was later dramatized in the acclaimed television series, *The Marvelous Mrs. Maisel*.

There was a plethora of performance venues: the Village Gate, the Bitter End, Bon Soir, Gaslight Café, Phase 2, Café Wha?, Commons, Upstairs at the Duplex, Café Au Go Go, and on and on. Many of these clubs had a weekly *hootenanny* where amateur musicians and comics performed for hours. Village club bookers would often select their regulars from these *hoots*. Nowadays hoots are known as open-mics (or just *mics*).

Just because you were a regular performer in the Village,

didn't necessarily mean you would get paid; some rooms would simply pass around the "breadbasket" and plead for donations. Another reason the Village was so appealing for rising comics was the proximity of real show business, just a few subway stops away in midtown Manhattan. Clubs like the Basin Street East and the Blue Angel booked touring comics and paid good money. Plus, bookers from *The Ed Sullivan Show*, *The Tonight Show*, and syndicated talk shows like *The Merv Griffin Show*, were scouring the clubs looking for the next Jonathan Winters or Dick Gregory.

As a result, comics migrated to the Village hoping to find their comedic voice and a ticket to fame. Among them: Bill Cosby from Philadelphia, Woody Allen from Brooklyn, Joan Rivers from Larchmont, Richard Pryor from Peoria, and George Carlin returning home from Dayton, Ohio with a wife and baby.

Within a few years all five of these budding stand-ups made it to *The Ed Sullivan Show*, and then so much more.

———

The first of the Village coffeehouse generation to break through was Bill Cosby. And it was a speedy ascent. Arriving in the summer of 1962, Cosby began performing regularly at the Gaslight Café. Fourteen months later he was doing his crowd-pleasing karate routine on *The Tonight Show*.

That initial TV appearance landed Cosby a record deal with Warner Bros. (Bob Newhart's label). His debut comedy album, *Bill Cosby Is A Very Funny Fellow... Right!* went platinum. It was the first in a string of immensely successful albums with names familiar to comedy record enthusiasts across the country.

- *I Started Out as A Child*
- *Why Is There Air?*

- *Wonderfulness*
- *Revenge*
- *To Russell, My Brother, Whom I Slept With*

In late 1964, it was announced that Bill Cosby would be the co-star of a new NBC television series, *I Spy*.

Woody Allen already had a lucrative comedy writing career when he was booked (for no money) by his managers into a small Village room called Upstairs at the Duplex. There he did two shows a night, six nights a week. For those who saw him at that time, it was often difficult to watch. Allen suffered from paralyzing stage fright, and he would often mumble his act or race through his routines, destroying any semblance of comedic timing. Allen would desperately clutch the microphone and stare at the ground because he was too petrified to make eye contact with the crowd.

But with his manager's patient encouragement, along with an uncommon work ethic combined with genius level joke-writing talent, Allen developed into a wildly original and influential comic. And it took him just a couple of years.

Soon he was playing other Village rooms like the Bitter End and Bon Soir, and even the city's midtown clubs. Allen eventually toured the country and appeared on most every television talk and variety show, including guest-hosting *The Tonight Show*. He recorded three comedy albums. And then, it was over. Allen abruptly quit stand-up in 1972, choosing instead to concentrate on his burgeoning filmmaking career.

There weren't many women stand-ups on the scene when Joan Rivers joined the fray: Jean Carroll, Moms Mabley, Totie Fields, and Phyllis Diller headed the list. The odds were long but Rivers was desperate to be famous. She tried everything to "make it." She began as an actress, then performed stand-up under the alias "Pepper January," emceed at a strip club, joined the Second City improv troupe, became part of a comedy trio, and even tried singing in her act.

Rivers was a grinder who worked diligently to learn how to get laughs. She was one of the first comics to audiotape her sets, dragging around a huge tape recorder to Village clubs like the Duplex and the Bitter End. And through sheer determination she became the comedic equal of those in the boys' club.

In February 1965, Rivers had a life-changing appearance on *The Tonight Show*. Instead of performing a stand-up set, she just bantered with Carson from the panel. She was vulnerable, charming, and hilarious. Carson was absolutely smitten and became her champion for the next twenty-one years. And Joan Rivers, who had dreamt of becoming an actress, performed stand-up comedy for the rest of her life.

When Richard Pryor first came to NYC, according to Scott Saul's biography, *Becoming Richard Pryor*, he went straight to the Apollo Theater in Harlem. But the Apollo bookers were not impressed with young Richard and they recommended that he try his luck in Greenwich Village. So, Pryor headed downtown and soon adapted the rhythm and delivery (and even some material) of Bill Cosby. The volatile, skinny comic performed at hoots and charmed the locals, eventually landing regular spots at several rooms. Manny Roth, the owner of Café Wha, saw huge mainstream potential in "Richie" Pryor and became his manager.

In 1964, a little more than a year after getting off the bus, Pryor made his network TV debut on ABC's *On Broadway Tonight*. He was introduced by radio legend Rudy Vallee. Then, in May 1965, Pryor made his first of over fifteen appearances on Ed Sullivan. Although it would take him several more years to completely shed the Cosby influence and find his own voice, Pryor was on his way.

When George Carlin arrived downtown, he already had late-night television experience (on Jack Paar's *Tonight Show*) as part of a comedy team (Burns and Carlin), and also as a comic impressionist. But his career had stalled, and he needed to provide for his wife and newborn.

Carlin made the decision to move back into his old apartment building in upper Manhattan and focus on developing a solid act that would get him to Hollywood, and into the movies. After a couple months of hootenannies, Carlin landed a sweet gig as the paid "house comic" at the Café Au Go Go. There he was able to workshop new material in a low-risk setting.

The Café Au Go Go provided Carlin with an environment that *showcase comedy clubs* would soon furnish for aspiring stand-ups; a performance lab where material could be honed until it was airtight and razor sharp.

Carlin had a very specific plan of action, he needed to build an act that could land him back on television. He found it in a routine called "The Indian Sergeant." That routine was his ticket. He was booked onto *The Merv Griffin Show* and quickly became a regular. Merv led to dozens of other TV bookings.

In mid-1966, George Carlin and Richard Pryor were hired to perform on the long-forgotten *Kraft Summer Music Hall* starring John Davidson. The two young comics went to Los Angeles for the gig. Both decided to stay in California for the rest of their lives, leaving behind NYC's coffeehouse and cabaret scene.

There were plenty of other aspiring comics working the Village in the early 1960s. Despite the creative and progressive atmosphere, it was actually a highly competitive environment. Acts like Stanley Myron Handelman, Steve Landesberg, Lily Tomlin, Howard Storm, David Brenner, Ron Carey, Gabe Kaplan, David Frye, Dick Cavett, Bob Altman (aka Uncle Dirty), David Steinberg, Larry Hankin, and even future indie director Henry Jaglom, all vied for stage time.

A café in Brooklyn, called Pip's, began utilizing *multiple comics* on the same show in 1962. But it was in a small room in midtown Manhattan where that idea really took hold. And, in just a few years, this midtown room would become the epicenter of the New York City stand-up comedy scene. And create an entertainment model that would spread across the USA, and then the world.

And it all happened quite by accident.

The seed for this stand-up revolution was planted when Gerson "Budd" Friedman and his wife Silver opened the Improvisation Café on West 44th Street in 1963. It was a dinky, Greenwich Village-style coffeehouse that could seat about 85 people. It didn't serve alcohol. Yet.

The Friedmans envisioned their tiny club/cafe as a hip hangout where Broadway performers could relax post-show and maybe sing for each other and the tourists. They set up a small stage with microphones and a piano. They didn't have the money to cover the back wall, it was just exposed brick.

Unlike Pip's, Budd Friedman had zero plans to feature comedians.

But fate intervened when, in 1964, a now largely forgotten nightclub comic named Dave Astor dropped in and performed a set for Budd and the crowd. It went so well that Astor returned the following night and brought some of his comedy buddies. Soon young Richard Pryor was stopping by, doing silly skits with Astor and his buddy Ron Carey. But it remained primarily a singer's room.

However that all changed as more and more New York comics showed up, crowding out the Broadway crooners and the beatnik poets. Budd Friedman encouraged this trend. Many comics he let onstage were nobodies, who trekked up from the

Village. While others, like Jackie Vernon, were legitimate night-club headliners. The Improvisation Café soon found its identity and became a *comedy room* – that also used singers.

Every night featured a lineup of multiple comedians, a concept whose time had come. The shows would go on hour after hour (often well past midnight) with Friedman's favorites getting the prime spots. This simple show-biz innovation marked the birth of the comedy club.

And the café became known as the Improv.

The Improv's success story was featured in magazine and newspaper profiles. This was something new: part comedy college, part club, part singles bar. The word was out. The Improv was the place for young stand-ups to learn their craft, find their "voice," and get discovered.

Rodney Dangerfield, a survivor from the Hanson's drugstore era, became the Improv's house emcee. But it was Robert Klein, arriving in 1966, who emerged as the club's first breakout star. The multi-talented Klein had a smart, keen, middle-class, observational style that became the template for the emerging comedy-club generation. Richard Lewis, Jay Leno, Paul Reiser, Larry Miller, Jerry Seinfeld, Bill Maher, and Jon Stewart all credit Robert Klein as their comedic guiding light.

While the Improv was nurturing another wave of comedians, there was still a large swath of show business that operated as it had before. The Catskills, Vegas, and the big nightclubs still existed but, as time clicked by, they offered entertainment geared more towards the Greatest Generation demographic. And even the comedy in those venues was changing.

A perfect example was the ascent of Buddy Hackett, who went from Borscht Belt tummler to Las Vegas star. Hackett brought *adult* stand-up comedy into the big showrooms of the Vegas strip. Suddenly the 600-seat Congo room of the Sahara Hotel was packed with tourists loving Hackett's off-color jokes. This wasn't expletive-laced comedy but more the tone of a dirty joke book.

Another addition to the old-school nightclub scene was the opening of a nationwide chain of Playboy Clubs (and resorts). These members-only rooms provided touring comics with lots of work but not too much money at the entry level.

Thanks to the television and record album success enjoyed by Bill Cosby, Moms Mabley, and Dick Gregory, the next wave of young African American comedians like Scoey Mitchell, Godfrey Cambridge, Irwin C. Watson, Stu Gilliam, and Flip Wilson were getting an opportunity to make their mark.

Flip Wilson, who had a breakthrough *Tonight Show* set with Carson in 1965 (thanks to an on-air recommendation from Redd Foxx), became a cultural icon when he starred in his own variety show for NBC.

In 1972, Flip Wilson graced the cover of *Time* magazine with the bold headline, "TV's First Black Superstar."

America's evolving comedy aesthetic was evident in two influential variety shows, both hosted by comedy teams, that debuted in the late 1960s. On CBS, *The Smothers Brothers Comedy Hour* was a satirical and topical program that pushed the boundaries of network censorship. Tom and Dick Smothers had developed their act in San Francisco at an 80-seat basement club called the Purple Onion (Phyllis Diller was also discovered there). Their TV show used an eclectic writing staff that included Rob Reiner, Murray Roman, Carl Gottlieb, Bob Einstein, and Steve Martin.

Meanwhile, NBC bet their money on Rowan and Martin, an

old-school, tuxedo-clad duo from the nightclub generation. Dan Rowan and Dick Martin had sharpened their act at renowned supper clubs like Chicago's Chez Paree, L.A.'s Coconut Grove, and NY's Copacabana. They were a surprising choice to host *Laugh-In*, a counterculture burlesque show that famously brought jump-cut editing to primetime. But it all somehow worked. And, in a foreshadowing of the comedy world to come, one of *Laugh-In's* young writers was Lorne Michaels.

Los Angeles had its own comedy scene. There were a number of rooms, primarily small music venues, that provided stage time for aspiring stand-ups. Clubs like The Ice House, the Horn, Ye Little Club, the Ash Grove, Bla-Bla Café, Ledbetter's, and the Troubadour used performers such as Pat Paulsen, Steve Martin, Paul Mooney, Alan Bursky, Lotus Weinstock, Murray Roman, Kelly Monteith, Franklyn Ajaye, Murray Langston, and on occasion, Albert Brooks.

Then, in 1972, three events transpired which altered the stand-up landscape.

1. Catch A Rising Star, NY's second comedy club, opened on the Upper East Side.
2. The Comedy Store, L.A.'s first comedy club, opened on Sunset Boulevard.
3. Johnny Carson moved NBC's *Tonight Show* from New York City to Burbank, California.

With the opening of The Comedy Store and Catch A Rising Star, the comedy club concept began to duplicate itself. It was no longer a curiosity on West 44th Street. It was now a business model with potential for huge growth. It should be noted that

Catch also featured singers. Pat Benatar was discovered there. But very quickly the comics, led by David Brenner, became the main draw.

L.A.'s Comedy Store opened at a legendary location. It was in the very same building that, years earlier, housed the renowned supper club Ciro's.

Both the Store and Catch eventually attracted legions of fans happy to plunk down both a cover charge and a drink minimum just to watch a slate of virtually unknown talent.

New York City had been home to *The Tonight Show* since the program's inception back in 1954. Broadcasting from Studio 6-B, Carson had already helped launch the careers of Don Rickles, Flip Wilson, Joan Rivers, and David Brenner.

Moving *The Tonight Show* to Los Angeles only increased Carson's stature in show business. That's where movies and television were made. And, because the *Ed Sullivan Show* was finally cancelled, late-night was becoming even more influential. People stayed up to watch Johnny Carson, the "King of Late Night."

On Thursday December 6, 1973, a year after the move west, Carson gave a memorable demonstration of his new power. After interviewing Diane Keaton and Sammy Davis Jr., Carson began his introduction of a young comic making his *Tonight Show* debut:

> *"He works in New York at the Improvisation and a place called Catch A Rising Star... would you welcome Freddie Prinze."*

And out walked a 19-year-old Prinze. What happened over the next fifteen minutes became the stuff of legend.

The self-assured Prinze caught fire as bit after bit elicited huge laughs and applause. That alone would have been a major triumph for any comic's first *Tonight Show*. But at the conclusion of his set, Prinze, instead of exiting behind the curtain, was waved over to the desk to have a follow-up conversation with Carson – an ultra-rare endorsement. And Prinze's appearance didn't stop there.

When the show returned from commercials, Prinze was *still sitting on the panel* as both Carson and Sammy Davis continued to gush over him.

Then, after another commercial break, Carson bumped the show's final guest (author Erma Bombeck) to talk a *third time* with the charismatic young comic. It was like something out of a dream.

A jazzed Carson declared after watching Prinze crush:

> *"There is no greater thrill for me personally than to have somebody come out here, who's unknown, and stand up in front of an audience and absolutely wipe 'em out with their first appearance, coast to coast."*

And that was the moment.

Showcasing young comics was now Carson's stated passion. Within a year of his stunning *Tonight Show* debut, Freddie Prinze was a millionaire and starring on the NBC sitcom *Chico and the Man*. It was now crystal clear. The pathway to fame and fortune ran straight through NBC's Studio 1 in Burbank.

Comics from across the land began their pilgrimage. Jay Leno from Massachusetts, David Letterman from Indiana, Jim Carrey from Toronto, Keenen Ivory Wayans from New York, Robin Williams from San Francisco, and Garry Shandling from Arizona were just a few of the thousands of comedians that descended on Los Angeles.

And they all dreamed of a successful spot on *The Tonight Show*.

In just a few short years...

- A comedian would reach rock star status.
- A premium cable network would allow comics total artistic freedom.
- A late-night variety show on Saturdays would begin its historic run.
- And an audacious comic would take stand-up comedy to new, creative heights.

7

HBO, SNL, AND PRYOR

Even when I was a little kid, I always said I would be in the movies one day. And damned if I didn't make it.

— RICHARD PRYOR

IN 1973, just as the youth culture was flexing its power, the New York Telephone Company recorded old-school stand-up Henny Youngman, "King of The One-Liners," for their new *Dial-A-Joke* service. When the service went live, it was a monster success as Youngman's concise, fast-paced jokes drew over three million calls during its first month of operation. Charging $1.50 the first minute, and 35¢ for each additional minute, it created a massive financial windfall for the utility. The 67-year-old Youngman was a cultural anomaly; he broke through back in 1937 on Kate Smith's radio show.

At the same time, the NBC network was courting a younger demographic (and the advertisers they attracted) when they decided to extend their broadcast day by an hour, on Friday nights. Following the *Tonight Show*, they slotted in a music program called *The Midnight Special*. It aired, ironically, at 1am. Although pop acts and singer-songwriters appeared, the show leaned towards rock music. And it also gave valuable exposure to young comics.

Don Kirshner's Rock Concert, a syndicated program with a very similar format (music with the occasional comic) also debuted in 1973. Viewers of these two music shows were treated to early stand-up sets from Billy Crystal, Lily Tomlin, Jimmie Walker, David Letterman, Steve Martin, Jay Leno, Franklyn Ajaye, Richard Belzer, Elayne Boosler, Garry Shandling, Richard Lewis, Gallagher, George Wallace, Gary Mule Deer, and Steve Landesberg.

Young comics in the 1970s were also frequently showcased on syndicated daytime talk shows hosted by Della Reese, Dinah Shore, Virginia Graham, and the two most popular shows, Mike Douglas and Merv Griffin.

But none of these programs carried the star-making potential of an appearance on *The Tonight Show starring Johnny Carson*. The show was crucial for both aspiring comics and for NBC's financial health. Carson was generating nearly sixty million dollars *a year* in revenue for the network. The show had hit its stride; it was profitable, popular, and relevant. In fact, the network aired a "best of" Carson at 11:30pm on Saturday nights.

In 1974, during his twelfth year as host, Carson wanted to scale back his workload to just four, and sometime three, nights a week. So, he proposed the network simply move the the *Best of Carson* from Saturday night to Monday night. NBC, desperate to keep their "golden goose" happy, obliged.

That left Saturday night, at 11:30, on NBC, wide open. And that's where 30-year-old showrunner Lorne Michaels stepped in.

Thanks to Carson's desire for a more relaxed work schedule, NBC launched Lorne Michaels' *Saturday Night Live* (originally called NBC's *Saturday Night*) in October of 1975.

Although no stand-ups were regular cast members at the outset, four out of the first seven hosts were comedians – George Carlin, Robert Klein, Richard Pryor, and Lily Tomlin. Great writing and casting, a perfect timeslot, and a new cultural permissiveness, all conspired to make the show a must-see event for comedy fans. The show's edgy, irreverent tone was completely in sync with the emerging Baby Boom generation, a demographic that, in 1975, didn't have a single member who had reached the age of 30. This wasn't your dad's variety show.

SNL's content was still constrained by both NBC's internal network standards and the Federal Communications Commission. So, when Richard Pryor hosted the show on December 13, 1975, NBC was so concerned about possible obscenities that it utilized a seven-second delay, giving nervous censors a brief window to bleep out any offensive words.

Seventeen days after Pryor hosted *Saturday Night* (almost) *Live*, an upstart pay channel gave over an hour of *uncensored* airtime to 33-year-old Robert Klein. Taped at Haverford College in Pennsylvania, it marked HBO's first stand-up special. And it would be a game changer.

Just three years before Klein's special aired, George Carlin was arrested in Milwaukee for using profanity on stage. And Richard Pryor had been arrested for obscenity in Richmond, Virginia in 1974.

Comics having to navigate local censorship laws was just a normal aspect of the job. Comedian and social critic Lenny Bruce was famously arrested several times for "speech crimes" in San Francisco, Chicago, Los Angeles, and New York City. The resulting criminal trials sent Bruce into a career and creative tailspin, culminating in a fatal drug overdose. But it sure didn't start with Lenny Bruce. Back in 1927, the double-entendre comedienne and actress, Mae West, spent *eight days in prison* following her conviction on obscenity charges in New York City.

A positive *New York Times* review of Robert Klein's HBO special helped convince the network to produce a series of stand-up specials that they called *On Location*. Surprisingly, a number of the next batch of specials were filled by old school headliners like Phyllis Diller, Myron Cohen, Totie Fields, George Kirby, and Pat Cooper.

HBO wanted Freddie Prinze for a stand-up special, but he told the network that he would prefer to just host a night of young comics. So, in late 1976, *On Location* went to the recently opened Hollywood Improv for a taping of *Freddie Prinze and Friends*. Bob Shaw, Jay Leno, Elayne Boosler, Tim Thomerson, and Gary Mule Deer rounded out the show.

The *Freddie Prinze and Friends* format became a prototype. It was simply a condensed version of a night at a comedy club hosted by a recognizable emcee. That template has been duplicated on television ever since.

HBO produced multiple specials using the *Freddie Prinze and Friends* motif, as well as two long-running stand-up series: *The Young Comedians Special* and *Def Comedy Jam*.

George Carlin joined the HBO team in March of 1977 with his first comedy special, taped at USC. He closed his set with an updated version of his famous routine, "The Seven Words You Can Never Say on Television." And now, here was George Carlin, for the very first time, saying *those words on television*.

HBO still had a relatively small number of subscribers compared to the broadcast networks, so the early *On Location* specials weren't career-defining moments. That was still to come.

Carlin's prodigious writing skills and curious mind were a perfect match for HBO's free speech zone. Over the rest of his career, Carlin created a new hour of comedy about every two years. He ultimately taped fourteen HBO specials.

In Newport Beach, California, an actual road comedy club called the Laff Stop, was up and running. It booked comedians for a week of shows and also housed them in a condominium. One early Laff Stop booking, in 1977, featured David Letterman, followed by Robin Williams, followed by Jay Leno.

Robin Williams was a wild improvisational comic in the mold of Jonathan Winters. He cut his teeth in San Francisco, not at the old Purple Onion or the hungry i, but at a small "club-house" room called the Holy City Zoo. The Zoo was part of an exploding San Francisco comedy club scene which would eventually include the Punch Line, the Other Café, and Cobb's.

Rumblings of a coming comedy boom were in the air.

Saturday Night Live's expanding cultural influence was on full display when it helped propel Steve Martin, who guest-hosted five times over two seasons, into the comedic stratosphere. Martin's quirky talents fit the show like a glove and the convergence helped turbocharge his career.

Not since the days when Milton Berle captivated millions on the *Texaco Star Theater* had a comedian burned so brightly. Martin had two gold comedy albums, a hit song ("King Tut"), a best-selling book (*Cruel Shoes*), and a string of sold-out concert arenas all across the land. Martin was now performing in venues that also booked Led Zeppelin.

This was something new. Stand-up comedy had its first rock star.

Steve Martin's act was entirely different from the satirical and political comics of the time. Basically, Martin made fun of being a "professional comedian." It was meta-comedy. He played a bumbling, narcissistic entertainer whose lack of self-awareness was fortified with an unshakable self-confidence. His "ramblin' guy" was both silly and subversive, and it went a long way to winning Steve Martin a Mark Twain Prize.

Martin's comedy hero was Wally Boag, the first comedian he ever saw perform live. Boag was a charismatic comic, balloon artist, gun spinner, and eccentric dancer. Born in 1920, he played small-time vaudeville and burlesque venues, entertained President Franklin Roosevelt, appeared in nightclubs, did a few Sullivan spots, and then spent over 25 years performing five shows a day at Disneyland's Golden Horseshoe Revue. That's where 10-year-old Steve Martin first caught Boag's crowd-pleasing antics.

As Steve Martin was packing concert arenas with an ocean of superfans wearing nose glasses, bunny ears, and arrows-through-their-heads; Village comic Woody Allen was winning multiple Oscars for writing and directing the Best Picture of 1977, *Annie Hall*. Just five years earlier, Allen was in Las Vegas, at Caesar's Palace, performing stand-up comedy.

Another veteran of the Village and NY's Improv, Lily Tomlin brought her one-woman show, *Appearing Nitely*, to Broadway in 1977. She was presented a special Tony Award (to go along with her three Emmys and a Grammy). Her theatrical show had elements of stand-up, but she was more in the tradition of monologist Ruth Draper, presenting a series of characters.

The hilariously inventive Tomlin made the cover of *Time*. The magazine anointed her the "New Queen of Comedy."

For those comics toiling in the trenches, the late '70s still provided many opportunities. One curious show, *The Comedy Shop*, was the first syndicated television show that featured just stand-ups and guest celebs to introduce them. Comics weren't sandwiched between music acts, or brought out in the last segment of a talk show, or asked to make one person laugh on a game show.

The Comedy Shop was hosted by Norm Crosby, a comic who specialized in malaprops ("They gave me a standing ovulation"). *The Comedy Shop*, perhaps more than any stand-up show in history, presented a fascinating cultural divide. For comedy fans it was both jarring and intriguing to watch nightclub, Vegas, and Catskill mainstays like Jackie Kahane, Jan Murray, Guy Marks, Sal Richards, Morty Gunty, Freddie Roman, Jackie Gayle, and Corbett Monica doing sets on the same shows with bright-eyed comedy-clubbers like Bob Saget, Mike Binder, Marsha Warfield, Brad Garrett, Mike Preminger, Arsenio Hall, Bobby Slayton, and Kevin Nealon.

On November 24, 1978, Comedy Store regular David Letterman made his stand-up debut on *The Tonight Show starring Johnny Carson*. And, in what has to be fastest ascent the show's history, Letterman was guest-hosting, just two months later.

Around this time, Letterman lent his name, and stature, to a comedians' strike at the Comedy Store. The issue was simple. The comics wanted to get paid. They figured if clubs were going to collect a cover charge for entertainment – the actual *entertainers* should get a cut of that money.

The Store, like other showcase comedy clubs in New York and L.A. didn't pay anything when they first opened up. Instead, they offered up free drinks. These rooms were considered *workshops* where talent could be nurtured and then discovered. Like what had happened to Jimmie Walker, Freddie Prinze, David Brenner, Gabe Kaplan, Robin Williams, and David Letterman.

But as the clubs became more popular, and lucrative, the comics took a stand. After a bitter conflict that lasted six weeks, the comedians won the day. The Comedy Store strike had a lasting impact on the livelihood of comics and helped lay the foundation for the '80s comedy boom. The precedent was set. Comedians were to be paid. The full saga of the strike was chronicled in *I'm Dying Up Here*, a 2009 book by *Los Angeles Times* reporter William Knoedelseder.

———

In a decade filled with remarkable stand-up milestones and achievements, one may stand above the rest: the film, *Richard Pryor: Live in Concert*.

Pryor had a major advantage over other comics working in the late 1970s... he was already a movie star. Like Bob Hope, Danny Kaye, Red Skelton, Jerry Lewis, and Woody Allen before him, he had successfully parlayed his persona into big screen success.

In 1978 alone, Pryor starred in three studio films: *Blue Collar, California Suite,* and *The Wiz.* But Pryor dreamed of releasing a full-length motion picture of his stand-up act. He had first tried back in 1971, but the result, a performance film called *Alive and Smokin'*, was deemed a disaster and never released theatrically.

However, this time, it would be different. He developed his new act at the Comedy Store with the input of his trusted accomplice, comedian Paul Mooney. Pryor called his onstage writing process "woodshedding." He then toured the country, sharpening the material at large theaters like DC's Kennedy Center, NY's City Center, and L.A.'s Pantages Theatre.

Then, over two nights in late December 1978, Pryor filmed his new act at the 3,100-seat Terrace Theater in Long Beach. Director Jeff Margolis caught lightning in a bottle. Pryor was at his creative peak and brimming with confidence.

The unrated film arrived in movie theaters just thirty-five days after it was shot. And for those who saw it, it was a revelation. Andrew Sarris, the legendary *Village Voice* film critic, wrote that watching *Richard Pryor: Live in Concert* was, "One of the most exhilarating experiences of my movie-going life."

Pryor, who began his TV career in 1964, wearing a suit and tie, while doing squeaky-clean Bill Cosby inspired material, had undergone a staggering transformation. Drawing inspiration from Lenny Bruce and Redd Foxx; his profane, satirical, and confessional tour-de-force brought stand-up comedy into the promised land.

The film *Live in Concert* is a large part of the reason that Richard Pryor is still considered, in poll after poll, the greatest stand-up ever.

As the 1970s came to a close, no one could have predicted the comedy tidal wave that was about to crash over American pop culture. In the next decade hundreds of comedy clubs would rise up, stand-up programming would saturate cable TV, a whole comedy industry would emerge, and two self-assured young comics from Long Island would become legends.

8

THE BOOM

To me, my whole life is a vacation. I have more fun when I'm working than when I'm not working. I get paid to joke around.

— JERRY SEINFELD

IN 1980, at age fifty-nine, stand-up comic Rodney Dangerfield was about to experience one of the great third acts in show business history. His surprising performance in the film *Caddyshack* made him a bankable movie star. Dangerfield was a grinder from another era. And it was finally paying off. He would star in several film comedies, host SNL, make commercials, win a Grammy Award (for *No Respect*), and host a few HBO specials.

It was a remarkable turnaround for a comic who had started in 1940 under the name Jack Roy and struggled for decades. Things got so dire that, at one point, he gave up his dream and hustled aluminum siding for a living. He reinvented himself as Rodney Dangerfield, and with his twitchy stage demeanor he learned to overpower a room with a non-stop barrage of one-liners each centered on the fact that he was a complete and total loser.

Dangerfield's signature dark suit, white shirt, and red tie now reside at the Smithsonian Institution in Washington, DC.

Meanwhile, Budd Friedman's accidental multi-comic show innovation was spreading across the country like a venereal disease. Before the decade was out, hundreds of new clubs would emerge, providing aspiring comics an income (often cash) and valuable stage time. Journalists would identify this era as the Comedy Boom.

These new comedy clubs were primarily converted live music venues, restaurants, movie theaters, nightclubs, discos, break rooms, bowling alleys, bars, and hotel conference rooms. They would present, depending on the local demand, a full week of shows, just weekends, or some combination of the two. A Wednesday through Sunday booking was very common.

Individual comedy nights, known as "one-nighters," also popped up like weeds.

Whether it was a plush 300-seater or a cramped banquet room in the corner of a Chinese restaurant, most of these rooms required four things.

1. A liquor license.
2. Access to talent.
3. A working microphone system.
4. Tables and chairs.

The sale of alcohol was the economic locomotive of the comedy club explosion. Several club owners were genuine stand-up aficionados, but they were the exception. Overwhelmingly these venues existed to sell booze and maybe some bar food. So, any venue that already had a liquor license, which in certain regions still meant a mob association, became a potential location for a new club. Most full-time comedy clubs required both a cover charge and an alcohol minimum (usually two drinks) for attendees.

The interstate highway system, cheap gas, and low-cost air travel facilitated the whole enterprise. Just as the railroads had once made the vaudeville circuit possible.

The names of these clubs evolved. The first comedy club, the

Improvisation, had an ironic name for a room that presented acts performing carefully written comedy material.

None of the old clubs in the '60s Village scene (The Bitter End, Village Gate, Gaslight, Duplex, Café Au Go Go) or in San Francisco (hungry i, Purple Onion, Ann's 440) had comedy-centric names. Pip's, the famed Brooklyn comedy room, was named after a character from the novel *Great Expectations*.

However, with the opening of the Comedy Store and the Laugh Factory in L.A., along with NY's Comic Strip and then later, Stand Up NY, the idea took hold that a humor-implied name might be a smart branding strategy. And so, it began.

Some of the boom-era clubs used very direct names: Richmond Comedy Club, Cleveland Comedy Club, Pittsburgh Comedy Club, Virginia Beach Comedy Club, Cobb's Comedy Club, Comedy and Magic Club, Houston Comedy Workshop, Austin Comedy Workshop.

Then some went in for a slightly more creative variation: Comedy Castle, Comedy Cottage, Comedy Asylum, Comedy Cabaret, Comedy Cellar, Comedy Connection, Comedy Corner, Komedy Korner, Comedy Workshop, Comedy Den, Comedy Outlet, Comedy Factory Outlet, Comedy Underground, Comedy Stop, Comedy Act Theater, Constant Comedy, Comedy Works, Comedy U., Comedy Zone, and (of course) Comedy Womb.

And finally, the fun/humiliating: Jokers, Giggles, Tickles, Chuckles, Rascals, Bonkerz, Zanies, Stitches, Crackers, Yuk Yuk's, Punch Line, Slapstix, Laff Stop, Wiseguys, Acme, Bananas, Hilarities, Coconuts, Mr. Rips, Sir Laughs-A-Lot, Laughing Stock, Funny Bone, Funny Farm, Funny Firm, Uncle Funny's, and Barrel of Laughs.

A few comedy club brands were franchised with multiple locations. So, comics could work just the Funny Bones or the Improvs or the Comedy Zones. There were also several comedy *runs* that stitched together a multi-week driving tour of small clubs and bars. The two most popular runs were the Comedy Caravan that included the Midwest and parts of the South – and the notorious Tribble Run that snaked through Idaho, Montana, Washington, Oregon, Wyoming, Nevada, and Colorado. As of 2021, the Tribble Run still exists and is seen by many road comics as a rite of passage.

Comedy clubs quickly settled into a standardized show lineup: Emcee/opener (12 minutes), middle/feature (25 minutes), and then the headliner (50+ minutes). With announcements, there was your 90-minute show.

These clubs were selling "comedy." You had to get laughs. That was the gig. It was right there on the sign. And so a lot of road comics fell into a dependable, crowd-pleasing lane. Many had skinny ties and interchangeable comedic observations.

The era also produced creative "character comedians" who filtered their bits through surreal, outsized personalities. Gilbert Gottfried, Bobcat Goldthwait, Andrew Dice Clay, Judy Tenuta, and Emo Philips led this brigade.

The expanding proliferation of comedy clubs also created a huge unintended benefit: local comedy scenes.

Every city with a comedy club had its own homegrown ecosystem for developing new talent. Acts could stay close to home while garnering valuable stage time as emcees or middle/feature acts before making their pilgrimage to NYC or L.A. in search of television exposure.

The story kept repeating itself in city after city.

- Bill Hicks in Houston
- Arsenio Hall in Chicago
- Dennis Miller in Pittsburgh
- Roseanne Barr in Denver
- Dave Chappelle in Washington, D.C.
- Sam Kinison in Austin

There were also scores of excellent comics that congregated in the two most comedically fertile breeding grounds of the era: San Francisco and Boston.

It seemed like the whole city of San Francisco embraced the '80s comedy boom. Besides multiple comedy clubs and theaters, promoters staged an annual stand-up competition that attracted eager comics from all across the country. The city also proclaimed an official Comedy Day complete with a free outdoor concert that attracted tens of thousands of spectators.

While Boston had a perfect storm for the boom: working class townies combined with thousands of brainy college students. It created a wild, boisterous comedy scene that was teeming with drugs, cash, sex, and alcohol.

One such local comedian was 26-year-old Steven Wright who, by the early '80s, had been performing in Boston at the Comedy Connection, Constant Comedy, and the Ding Ho (Chinese restaurant/comedy club) for several years.

In 1982, *Tonight Show* executive producer Peter Lassally, in town to check out colleges for his kids, dropped by to see a show. After a night of watching the local talent, he thought just one Boston comic might be ready for network television. A couple weeks later, Steven Wright got the call – they wanted him on the *Tonight Show*.

On Friday night, August 6, 1982, Wright walked through the curtain of NBC's Studio 1, and grabbed the microphone out of its stand. Over the next six minutes he proceeded to live the dream of every young comic in America: a wildly successful debut set on Carson.

Wright was then summoned over to the couch. There, in a stunned daze, he tried to answer Carson's questions. He even managed to mention his Boston crew back at the Comedy Connection. Wright was immediately rebooked and made his second *Tonight Show* appearance the *very next week*.

That's how quickly it could happen.

"It changed my entire experience as a human being on this planet," Steven Wright explained years later in the definitive Boston comedy scene documentary, *When Stand Up Stood Out*.

To be clear, there were also hundreds of comics who made it all the way to Carson's *Tonight Show* – whose lives on the planet were not significantly transformed. Many even did multiple spots, raised their "quote" for road gigs, and enjoyed the admiration of family, friends, and colleagues. For those, appearing on *The Tonight Show* was certainly a career dream fulfilled but, ultimately, just an impressive credit for their introduction.

In 1982, NBC began broadcasting another talk show, *Late Night with David Letterman*. It aired after Carson, at 12:30am. The irreverent show became an additional opportunity for comics to reach a younger demographic and also boost their appearance fees. The most utilized stand-ups on *Letterman* were Richard Lewis, Carol Leifer, George Miller, Sandra Bernhard, and Jay Leno.

Two comics from Long Island, Eddie Murphy and Jerry Seinfeld, experienced the decade in very different ways.

Murphy's rise was absolutely stunning. As a teenager, possessed with uncommon confidence, he was cast on *Saturday Night Live*. He became the show's breakout star and is credited with saving the franchise. He recorded his debut comedy album, *Eddie Murphy*, at NY's Comic Strip. It, of course, went gold and scored Murphy a Grammy nomination. Then he landed a few successful *Tonight Show* appearances. He starred in three motion pictures – *48 Hours, Trading Places,* and *Beverly Hills Cop* – as well as taping his first stand-up special. This all happened to Murphy *before* the age of 25.

No other comic had ever ascended so quickly. The only close comparison was Jerry Lewis (one of Murphy's idols) who, as a 20-year-old, exploded onto the comedy scene in 1946 when he teamed up with singer Dean Martin.

Eddie Murphy's most notable stand-up legacy might be his first comedy special, *Delirious*, filmed at Washington DC's Constitution Hall. Inspired by Pryor's *Live in Concert*, it became a must-see event and was a huge success for HBO whose subscription base had ballooned in the early '80s. For a generation of young comedians that followed, *Delirious*, was their inspiration.

Jerry Seinfeld followed a more traditional path. In 1981, after a successful *Tonight Show* debut, he was cast in a supporting role on the NBC sitcom, *Benson*. But, unlike Eddie Murphy, he had trouble acting. Seinfeld was fired after just three episodes. At that point he decided that if he were ever given a chance to act on television again – that he would have to be in control of the scripts.

Seinfeld became a national comedy headliner, and a legend among young stand-ups for his savant-like observational skills, blue-collar work ethic, and airtight joke construction. He was a machine.

Most acts at that time had a dual-track creative process; construct a series of clean, precise, five-minute "sets" that were suitable for television – while simultaneously compiling a more R-rated "act" for the road. With Seinfeld, it was all one track. He never had to clean up a routine for network television.

The increasing influence of HBO was evident on August 3, 1985 when Rodney Dangerfield hosted the *9th Annual Young Comedians Special*. The nine comics who performed that evening were Harry Basil, Richie Gold, Bob Saget, Rita Rudner, Maurice

Lamarche, Bob Nelson, Yakov Smirnoff, Louie Anderson, and an ex-Pentecostal evangelist from Texas, named Sam Kinison.

HBO executives did not want the boundary-pushing Kinison on the program. But they ran into an immovable object named Rodney Dangerfield. He was crazy about Kinison and was adamant that he be included in the taping.

And so, following the comedy stylings of Yakov Smirnoff, Sam Kinison hit the stage and launched into his primal scream observations about women, marriage, and the famine in Africa. There was nothing safe or conventional about Kinison. Both his material *and* his delivery were radical and wildly original. You felt Kinison.

That single HBO performance launched his national career.

Kinison's ascent was also boosted by successful sets on *Late Night with David Letterman* and *Saturday Night Live*. He was the first comic in many years to achieve national fame without the endorsement of an early *Tonight Show* appearance.

Even SNL wasn't immune to the cultural power of the comedy boom. The show hired stand-ups to perform *between* sketches, something they had first tried years earlier with Andy Kaufman.

In addition to Kinison, SNL gave airtime to Harry Anderson, Joel Hodgson, Steven Wright, Paula Poundstone, Steve Landesberg, Michael Davis, and Frankie Pace.

In 1985, SNL hired Dennis Miller, a stand-up, to anchor its Weekend Update segment.

The boom was in full swing and an entire industry was flourishing. According to the *New York Times*, more than a million Americans *a month* saw live comedy in 1986, and they ponied up over $500 million in drink purchases and cover charges. Some road headliners were now pulling down more than $10,000 a week, while still making just $20 a set at showcase clubs in L.A. and New York.

Major beer and alcohol companies jumped on board as corporate partners. It was a perfect fit. Miller Light, Budweiser, Coors Light, Sam Adams, and Johnny Walker all sponsored national and regional comedy competitions. Maxwell House Coffee used young comics in their TV ad campaigns. Chicklets Gum underwrote a college stand-up search.

GQ, Hollywood Reporter, and *Rolling Stone* magazines began publishing special comedy issues. Montreal's *Just for Laughs* Comedy Festival lifted their *ban* on English-speaking performers.

Then came *The Comedy Awards,* produced by George Schlatter, which began as a *primetime* network special on ABC. Agents, managers, bookers, club owners, TV execs, and publicists were all riding the comedy boom gravy train. New specialty magazines like *Rave, LaughTrack,* and *Comedy USA,* covered the scene.

Perhaps stand-up comedy's coming-of-age moment occurred in March of 1986, when Billy Crystal, Whoopi Goldberg, and Robin Williams co-hosted *Comic Relief,* an HBO special/telethon that raised money and awareness for the homeless. It was the comedy world's turn to step up for a cause – just as musicians had with *Live Aid* and *Farm Aid.*

For the event, HBO unblocked and shared its live feed from the Universal Amphitheater, allowing millions of basic cable viewers to watch over four hours of uncensored performances by comedians, sketch actors, and sitcom stars.

Although it had a smaller subscription base, Showtime was also a player in the "comedy special" game. Its first, and most prolific, performer was Gallagher (a veteran of HBO's *2nd Young Comedians Special*). Beginning in 1980, Gallagher created fourteen specials for the network. He amassed a huge, dedicated fan base, as he headlined arenas and theaters throughout the boom years and beyond.

Showtime also gave early specials to Richard Jeni, Jim

Carrey, Tim Allen, Joan Rivers, Richard Lewis, Carol Leifer, Garry Shandling, Mike McDonald, Paul Reiser, and Denis Leary. Elayne Boosler was especially productive, she starred in four Showtime stand-up specials over five years.

Showtime also produced event programming: *The Comedy and Magic Club's 10th Anniversary, Funniest Person in America, Second City's 15th Anniversary Special,* and *The First Aspen Comedy Festival.*

In the middle of America's embrace of young comedians, an Ed Sullivan-era shlepper had the most unlikely and spectacular comeback. In December of 1986, Jackie Mason opened his one-man show, *The World According to Me!,* on Broadway. It became the surprise hit of the season, garnering Mason stellar reviews and a special Tony Award. It went on to become the most successful one-person Broadway show since comedian/pianist Victor Borge's record-setting run back in the 1950s.

Mason parlayed his stage success into a starring role in *Caddyshack II* and a new ABC sitcom called *Chicken Soup.* The network was hoping Mason would become the latest in a long line of comedians to turn onstage success into television sitcom gold. *Chicken Soup* didn't last long but it seemed like a good bet.

Since the birth of television, comedians have been able to successfully transition to the small screen. They have an advantage over most actors. Comedians come armed with a market-tested persona, performance skills, and a sense of comedic timing. It's been true in every decade.

- The '50s: Jackie Gleason, Wally Cox, Danny Thomas, and Phil Silvers.
- The '60s: Andy Griffith/Don Knotts, Joey Bishop, Phyllis Diller, Bill Dana, Jerry Van Dyke, Sandy Baron, and Don Adams.
- The '70s: Bob Newhart, Redd Foxx, Freddie Prinze, Jimmie Walker, Gabe Kaplan, Steve Landesberg, Billy Crystal, and Robin Williams.

The '80s were no different. *The Cosby Show*, an NBC ratings sensation, was credited with saving the situation comedy. On its heels came Bob Saget and Dave Coulier (*Full House*), Paul Reiser (*My Two Dads*), Garry Shandling (*It's Garry Shandling's Show*), Harry Anderson and Marsha Warfield (*Night Court*), Richard Lewis (*Anything but Love*), and Roseanne Barr with her 1988 runaway hit, *Roseanne.*

But most aspiring comics in New York and L.A. during the boom years never starred in a sitcom or received a lucrative network development/holding deal. They just played *clubs and colleges*; auditioned for acting roles; and picked up various gigs: corporate, cruise ships, benefits, birthdays, audience warm-up, temples and churches, and even traffic school instructing.

One distinctive characteristic that defined the comedy boom era was the enormous glut of televised *stand-up shows* featuring a slate of eager young comics doing eight minutes from their act.

For example, just in the year 1989... Tim Allen, Judd Apatow, Louis C.K., Ellen DeGeneres, Jeff Garlin, Gilbert Gottfried, Bill Hicks, Martin Lawrence, Norm Macdonald, Chris Rock, Ray Romano, Brian Regan, Adam Sandler, David Spade, Jon Stewart,

Damon Wayans, and Larry Wilmore all performed on one of these five stand-up shows:

1. A&E's *An Evening at the Improv*
2. MTV's *Half-Hour Comedy Hour*
3. VH1's *Stand-up Spotlight*
4. Fox's *Comic Strip Live*
5. Fox's *Comedy Express*

Stand-up shows were easy and cheap to produce, they got decent ratings, and most utilized the old *Freddie Prinze and Friends* formula.

And they were everywhere: *Caroline's Comedy Hour, Comedy Tonight, Good Time Café, Rascals Comedy Hour, Comedy Club Network, Comedy Club All-Stars, Sunday Funnies, Comedy on the Road, George Schlatter's Comedy Club, Triple Clowns, Sunday Comics, Full Frontal Comedy,* and on and on and on.

You would think that might be enough televised stand-up – but not even close.

Boom-era comics were also booked on talent competition shows like *Star Search* and *The Big Laff Off*; music programs like *American Bandstand, Soul Train, Showtime at The Apollo,* and *Solid Gold*; music video compilation shows such as *Night Flight* and *Friday Night Videos*; and even news programs like *The CBS Morning News*.

HBO presented its first all-black (with the exception of Barry Sobel) stand-up special entitled *Uptown Comedy Express*, and also produced four all-female specials called *Women of The Night*. Then, in 1989, they began a new series of stand-up *half-hours* that they branded *One Night Stand*.

If you wanted your comedy on demand, you could purchase home video compilations like *Big City Comedy, Dirty Dirty Jokes,*

New Wave Comedy, or the *Paramount Home Theater* (you can see future-director Paul Feig on volume two of this VHS series).

By the end of the '80s, the power of *The Tonight Show* was finally beginning to fade. Carson had awarded a new generation of stand-ups including Keenen Ivory Wayans, Garry Shandling, Jim Carrey, Ellen DeGeneres, Louie Anderson, Roseanne Barr, and Kevin Pollak his coveted seal-of-approval. But, more and more, it was the ironic and sarcastic *Late Night with David Letterman,* at 12:30am, that captured the era's comedic zeitgeist. Plus, the growing success of *The Arsenio Hall Show* chipped away at Carson's late-night supremacy.

Large media corporations decided it was time to cash in on the comedy boom. The cable television landscape included movie channels, sports channels, a kids' channel, 24-hour news channels, and a music video channel. So why not a comedy channel? Or two?

What ensued was a titanic battle between Time-Warner (HBO's parents) and Viacom (MTV's folks) to create America's first all-comedy cable channel.

This is how it went down. The Time-Warner bankrolled Comedy Channel got to market first, on November 15, 1989. But about four months later, on April 1 (someone's thinking!), Viacom jumped into the fray with their all-comedy channel called HA!

Unfortunately, with an excess of stand-up shows already crowding the marketplace, it soon became evident that there weren't enough comedy fans to sustain both networks. The Comedy Channel and HA! started bleeding money.

So, after a year of intense negotiations, the two networks merged, and The Comedy Network was born. *The Comedy Network*? Due to a naming conflict with a Canadian show, The Comedy Network was quickly rebranded as Comedy Central.

Comedy Central was hoping to be the MTV for comedians, looking to break the next Seinfeld, Leno, Roseanne, or Eddie Murphy.

The comedy boom chugged into the next decade. Andrew Dice Clay was touring the country playing huge sports arenas filled with wild and raucous fans. They often chanted along, in unison, with his signature adult nursery rhymes. In February 1990, Clay sold out New York's Madison Square Garden. He was the first stand-up comedian to accomplish that feat. The demand for tickets was so immense that Clay added a second night at MSG – which he also sold out.

In May and June of 1990, NBC aired four episodes of *Seinfeld*, a sitcom created by Jerry and Larry David. Seinfeld had devised a nifty work-around for his lack of acting chops when he portrayed a comedian named "Jerry Seinfeld" on the program. The show struggled for a time before becoming the #1 TV show in America and an enduring cultural touchstone.

But there was blood in the water. Comic Ritch Shydner, in his detailed exploration of the boom years, *Kicking Through the Ashes*, noticed that, around 1991, the comedy clubs began rolling back their fees. They also started allowing customers to bring in multiple guests – for free. The boom was about to bust.

Over the next decade, nearly half of all road work in the U.S. would dry up as hundreds of comedy rooms went belly up, including two of New York City's most iconic clubs: The Improv and Catch A Rising Star.

However, it wasn't all gloom or doom. There were several positive trends on the horizon.

- A new, alternative style of stand-up would emerge.
- The FOX TV network would trigger a wave of African American comedy programming.
- A flood of comedians got their own sitcoms.
- And, an impressionist/stand-up became the highest paid movie star in the world.

9

ALTERNATIVE AND URBAN

My only goal was to do a special that was good enough that when I played a club, I wouldn't have to promote it on radio.

— CHRIS ROCK

IN 1990, four young stand-ups, Adam Sandler, David Spade, Rob Schneider, and Chris Rock, joined NBC's *Saturday Night Live*. That very same year, over on FOX, a sketch show called *In Living Color* made its broadcast debut. It was the brainchild of comedian Keenen Ivory Wayans, and it featured stand-ups Damon Wayans, Kim Coles, Jim Carrey, Shawn Wayans, Tommy Davidson, and (later) Jamie Foxx.

Few would have predicted at the time that *In Living Color* would unleash an unprecedented wave of urban sitcoms, films, and new comedians. Or that Carrey and Sandler would become movie stars. Or that Chris Rock would film the most critically acclaimed stand-up special since Richard Pryor's *Live in Concert*.

Besides helping to kill off some comedy clubs, the explosion of stand-up shows on TV had another effect – customers at clubs began to expect what they saw at home: polished killer routines. One comic, Janeane Garofalo, felt like she couldn't meet those expectations. She hoped that, perhaps, there was an easier, friendlier way to present stand-up.

So, in the summer of 1991, with notebook in hand, she and her comedy pals (including Colin Quinn and Dana Gould) started doing sets at Big & Tall Books on Beverly Boulevard in Los Angeles. And although the gig lasted only a year at that location, it uncorked a new aesthetic in comedy for both performers and audiences.

What Garofalo started eventually became known as *alternative comedy*. It borrowed the idea from the music industry where some bands – college, underground, regional – were categorized as an alternative to mainstream popular music.

To be clear, prior to Garofalo's gang, there had been a long tradition of comedians whose style was alternative: Jack Gilford, Irwin Corey, Jonathan Winters, Lord Buckley, Dick Shawn, Brother Theodore, Andy Kaufman, Sandra Bernhard, and Neil Hamburger all performed creative nontraditional stand-up. And there have been comics and performance artists who did their shows outside the comedy clubs.

However, there was never a specific categorized scene until the 1990s. Audiences gave these comedians, who were performing in *alternative spaces*, wide latitude, encouraging them to avoid traditional comedy premises that were standard, crowd-pleasing fare at mainstream comedy clubs.

Hackneyed routines were sniffed out and shunned in these rooms.

Stand-up got less "jokey" and even more personal and experimental. The results ranged from painfully self-indulgent to comedically thrilling. It was stand-up for comedy fans – not drunk tourists steered into clubs by aggressive street teams hustling discount coupons. These new DIY comedy shows often bypassed traditional industry gatekeepers and opened new worlds of comedic invention.

Los Angeles music venues like Highland Grounds and the Diamond Club began attracting dedicated fans who were treated to the early work of Tenacious D and the first stage appearances of Bob Odenkirk and David Cross as a duo.

West Hollywood's LunaPark became the home of a highly popular Sunday night show, *UnCabaret*. The host (and booker), Beth Lapides, had one simple rule: comics were forbidden to use material from their "act." Lapides also creatively used an offstage mic to engage with performers like Judy Toll, Patton Oswalt, Andy Dick, Greg Behrendt, Margaret Cho, Julia Sweeney, and Taylor Negron. *UnCabaret* set the template for alt shows that continues today. They are usually once-a-week affairs overseen by the show's creators.

Improv actress turned stand-up Kathy Griffin hosted her own weekly alt show, *Hot Cup O' Talk*, at the Groundlings Theatre. The alt scene started small but would eventually have a profound influence on the tapestry of stand-up comedy.

As this alternative comedy revolution was brewing, the old-school mountain comedians took a victory lap. *Catskills on Broadway* opened at the Lunt-Fontaine Theater in late 1991 and featured Freddie Roman, Dick Capri, Marilyn Michaels, and the legendary Mal Z. Lawrence. The Borscht Belters ran for over a year on Broadway and then successfully toured the country. Later in the decade, numerous comedians adapted the four-comic template to create branded stand-up tours, films, specials, and home videos.

Just as the comedy boom was beginning to contract, a new comedy club opened in Chicago. It was called All Jokes Aside and, although it lasted less than ten years, its legacy still reverberates today. It was a black owned and operated club that stood at the epicenter of the '90s black stand-up wave.

In some ways, the club was study in contradictions. It booked edgy heavy hitters of the day like Jamie Foxx, Bernie Mac, Steve Harvey, and Adele Givens – while it was also a throwback to the posh nightclubs of the 1940s. All Jokes Aside instituted a strict dress code and comedians who "ran-the-light" (did more than their allotted time) were fined.

Even though Dick Gregory had broken the nightclub color line thirty years before All Jokes Aside opened, there was still a market for predominately black comedy rooms. Harlem had the Uptown Comedy Club, Miami had Studio 183, Atlanta had the Uptown Comedy Cabaret, and L.A. had the Comedy Act Theatre.

It was at the Comedy Act Theatre where Robin Harris gained his legendary reputation as the house emcee. Like Nipsey Russell at Club Baby Grand, Don Rickles at the Casbar lounge, or Richard Belzer at Catch A Rising Star – Robin Harris became the room's must-see attraction. He was something else – a fearless, lightning-fast improvisor who would insult regular customers or celebrities with the same ferocity. Just as his film career was starting to gain traction, Robin Harris died of a heart attack at age 36.

In 1992, Johnny Carson retired as host of *The Tonight Show*. After 30 years, the king's reign was over. It wasn't just that Carson provided young stand-ups with an opportunity to perform a set on national television. He, like *Tonight Show* hosts before him, allowed some of his favorite comedians to *host the program*. Woody Allen, Joey Bishop, David Brenner, George Carlin, Bill Cosby, Gabe Kaplan, Jay Leno, David Letterman, Jerry Lewis, Steve Martin, Bob Newhart, Don Rickles, Joan Rivers, Garry Shandling, David Steinberg, and Flip Wilson all guest-hosted the most popular show in late-night. That level of generosity, and professional confidence, is unheard of in the post-Carson television universe.

Carson's retirement also marked a generational shift. Carson grew up in pre-television America and first dreamt of getting laughs while listening to Fred Allen, Bob Hope, and Jack Benny on the radio (all three of those comics had their origins back in vaudeville). He was fascinated by their process and was obviously a "comedy nerd" decades before the phrase existed.

In 1949, while at the University of Nebraska, Carson's senior thesis was on radio joke writing and construction. He spliced together audio clips from monologues and explained his theories on how the laughs were generated. This type of scholarship and research foreshadowed a 21st century development when select colleges and universities began offering comedy as an accredited major.

With Carson out of the picture, two old Comedy Store friends, David Letterman and Jay Leno, battled it out to take over the *Tonight Show*. Leno ultimately prevailed but Letterman got a gold-plated consolation prize. He began hosting his own 11:30pm talk show on CBS – broadcast from the storied Ed Sullivan Theater in New York City. And a virtually unknown comedy writer, Conan O'Brien, took over Letterman's 12:30am NBC slot.

With the *Arsenio Hall Show* going strong in syndication, the comedy-club generation now owned late-night talk. The details of the titanic Leno-Letterman struggle were chronicled in *The Late Shift*, a book by *New York Times* journalist Bill Carter.

———

Martin Lawrence made a big splash in 1992, becoming the latest comic to star in his own sitcom, *Martin*. He was also hired as the host of HBO's new hip-hop infused stand-up show, *Def Comedy Jam*.

Over its many incarnations, *Def Comedy Jam* has showcased scores of African American comics including Bill Bellamy, Eddie Griffin, Sheryl Underwood, Katt Williams, Mo'Nique, Aries Spears, JB Smoove, Chris Tucker, and Tracy Morgan.

But perhaps no single *Def Comedy* performance was more compelling than Bernie Mac's second appearance on the show. Waiting backstage, Mac heard the raucous crowd relentlessly boo another comic. This set off Mac and when he finally hit the stage, he was focused and defiant. He stared down the crowd and declared: "I ain't scared of you mother..." This moment delighted the audience and made for some compelling theater. His punchlines were accented by DJ Kid Cupid's perfectly timed music drops. Throughout the now-legendary set, Mac kept calling back his opening mantra, "You don't understand. I ain't scared of you mother..."

Also, in 1992, *Comic View*, yet another stand-up show began its 16-year run on BET. It was first hosted by D.L. Hughley.

1992 also marked the debut of HBO's *The Larry Sanders Show*, an influential and ground-breaking, single-camera comedy. Co-created by and starring Garry Shandling, it brilliantly dramatized the neurotic backstage world of a late-night talk show. Shandling, a frequent guest-host of Carson's *Tonight Show*, knew this world quite well. Famous comedians, actors, and musicians were more than happy to appear on *Larry Sanders* as a *version* of themselves. The show also provided stand-up/writer Judd Apatow with his first directing assignment.

On October 1, 1993, comedian Bill Hicks taped an appearance on CBS's *Late Show with David Letterman*. Hicks, who came out of the Houston comedy scene, had made eleven successful appearances on Letterman's 12:30am NBC show. But there were different network expectations for a show that aired just an hour earlier, at 11:30pm.

After the taping, Letterman and his producers huddled up and decided to cut Hicks's entire set from the broadcast. They thought his material was just too controversial for the time slot. Hicks never got another chance to perform on Letterman. Just four months later he died of pancreatic cancer, at age 32.

In 2009, Letterman invited Hicks's mother, Mary, onto the show. He profusely apologized and then aired her son's banned stand-up set, in its entirety.

By 1994, both NYC's Improv (44th St. location) and Catch A Rising Star had closed their doors. It was shocking news. It was one thing for Cleveland's third comedy club to go under but the Improv? *GQ* magazine had once called it the "Yankee Stadium of comedy."

And the news of Catch A Rising Star going under was also alarming. What was happening? In its heyday Catch was known as the Studio 54 of comedy clubs. It had an A-list clientele with limousines often double-parked up and down 1st Avenue. Richard Belzer, their hip, quick-witted, house emcee had his own following. It was *the* hot room in New York. Plus, Catch's management seemed to have a smart, aggressive business strategy. They were the first comedy club to go public and issue shares on the NY Stock Exchange. Plus, they had successfully franchised satellite clubs into Las Vegas, Princeton, and Boston. There were plans to open another twenty-five Catch A Rising Star's across the country. Then, it was suddenly over.

"The Last Stand for Stand Up?" blazed the headline in a 1994 *Los Angeles Times* article.

"What killed the comedy business?" wondered writer Larry Doyle in his *New York* magazine cover story on the same subject.

There was real concern in the industry that this whole "comedy thing" might just go away.

Like disco.

Despite all the hand wringing, comedy clubs still existed across the country – just in smaller numbers. And there were multiple reasons offered up for the dramatic contraction.

1. *Economics.* Club owners thought the expansion would never end and over-saturated many markets.
2. *Greed.* Clubs upped their cover charge and drink prices. Live comedy was no longer a cheap evening. It was now more expensive than the movies.
3. *Atmosphere.* Clubs required that all customers buy two alcoholic drinks and the checks were dropped, and money collected, in the middle of the headliner's set. Plus, the moment a show ended, some clubs blared aggressive music in an effort to quickly "clear the room." This vibe left an unpleasant aftertaste for many fans.
4. *Television.* Fans could easily check out comics from the comfort of their living room couch. And Comedy Central only added to the glut with its own stand-up programing slate.

The industry was experiencing what economists describe as a market correction. Comedians who did tour, embraced new ways of monetizing their shows. Selling merchandise post-show, a tradition that goes back to nightclub performer Sophie Tucker, became even more commonplace. Self-produced CDs, DVDs, T-shirts, posters, and hats adorned merch tables near the exit, with hopeful comics standing at the ready with Sharpie, extra cash, and a credit-card swiper.

But many comedy-boom acts, once riding high during the frenzy, were forced out of performing. Some successfully transitioned to comedy writing, directing, advertising, or acting. Others ended up with day jobs.

It was especially tough for new comics, starting out in the early '90s, to gain footing. But for those already in the pipeline, it was the best of times; like a comic from Canada who started at Toronto's Yuk Yuk's Comedy Club – Jim Carrey.

In 1994, Carrey achieved what had to be the most head-spinning comedic accomplishment of the decade. In a single calendar year, he had three feature films open: *Ace Ventura: Pet Detective* (Feb. 4), *The Mask* (July 28), and *Dumb & Dumber* (Dec. 6). Together they grossed more than $700 million worldwide. After that unprecedented trifecta, Carrey commanded an eye-popping $20 million a movie. He became the highest paid actor in Hollywood. No stand-up comedian turned movie star, *before or since*, has so thoroughly dominated the box office.

Also, in 1994, Montreal's *Just for Laughs* Festival started their New Faces comedy showcase. It was an evening of undiscovered comics performing a high stakes audition in front of the "industry." The concept was successful out of the gate and became a critical element of the festival's programming. Since then, hundreds of *new faces* from Jimmy Fallon and Hasan Minhaj, to Ron Funches and Kate Berlant, have received a career boost at the yearly comedy fest.

Comic Tim Allen, who began in Detroit at the Comedy Castle, racked up his own impressive comedic feat in 1994. Allen had the nation's #1 television show (*Home Improvement*), the #1 book on the *New York Times* best-seller list (*Don't Stand Too Close to a Naked Man*), and the #1 motion picture (*The Santa Clause*), all in the same week.

Allen was part of a '90s avalanche of TV sitcoms starring stand-up comedians. NBC, CBS, and ABC were joined by upstart networks UPN, WB, and FOX in a mad scramble to find the next money-printing machine like *Seinfeld* or *Roseanne*.

Talent executives scoured the clubs. Comedy festivals like Aspen's *Comedy Arts Festival* and Montreal's *Just for Laughs* became feeding frenzies where comics were signed to development deals like never before.

The '90s *stand-up to sitcom* bonanza was absolutely massive. It included:

- *All-American Girl* (Margaret Cho)
- *Bless This House* (Andrew "Dice" Clay)
- *Boston Common* (Anthony Clarke)
- *Buddies* (Dave Chappelle)
- *Charlie Hoover* (Sam Kinison)
- *Common Law* (Greg Giraldo)
- *Costello* (Sue Costello)
- *Daddy Dearest* (Richard Lewis, Don Rickles),
- *Davis Rules* (Jonathan Winters, Tamayo Otsuki)
- *The Drew Carey Show*
- *The Ellen Show* (Ellen DeGeneres)
- *Everybody Hates Chris* (Chris Rock)
- *Everybody Loves Raymond* (Ray Romano, Brad Garrett)
- *The George Carlin Show*
- *Grace Under Fire* (Brett Butler)
- *The Good Life* (John Caponera)
- *Hangin' with Mr. Cooper* (Mark Curry)
- *Hiller and Diller* (Richard Lewis, Kevin Nealon)
- *Home Improvement* (Tim Allen)
- *The Hughleys* (D.L. Hughley)
- *The Jamie Foxx Show*

- *The Jeff Foxworthy Show*
- *On Our Own* (Ralph Harris)
- *The King of Queens* (Kevin James)
- *The Second Half* (John Mendoza)
- *Malcolm and Eddie* (Eddie Griffin)
- *Martin* (Martin Lawrence)
- *Morton and Hayes* (Kevin Pollak)
- *The Norm Show* (Norm Macdonald, Artie Lange)
- *Just Shoot Me* (David Spade)
- *Mad About You* (Paul Reiser)
- *The Parent 'Hood* (Robert Townsend)
- *Platypus Man* (Richard Jeni)
- *The Sinbad Show*
- *The Steve Harvey Show*
- *Unhappily Ever After* (Stephanie Hodge)
- *The Wayans Brothers* (Marlon and Shawn Wayans)

The above list contains only the shows that were actually broadcast. There's no telling how many unaired pilots and partially developed shows, with comics, that never saw the light of day.

By mid-decade the alternative comedy scene was gaining momentum on both coasts. The scene would reach its peak when two small music venues, nearly 3,000 miles apart, L.A.'s Largo and NY's Luna Lounge, hosted Monday night alt shows.

They both became packed, must-see events. Fans could catch creative sets from acts like Paul F. Tompkins, Patton Oswalt, Marc Maron, Janeane Garofalo, Maria Bamford, Todd Glass, Karen Kilgariff, Mitch Hedberg, Greg Behrendt, Mary Lynn Rajskub, and Andy Kindler.

Something was definitely happening and the entertainment industry, as well as the media, took notice. HBO greenlit David Cross and Bob Odenkirk's *Mr. Show*. The inventive program, inspired in part by *Monty Python's Flying Circus*, brought a post-modern sensibility to sketch television.

On May 31, 1996, the *New York Times* declared that Luna Lounge's Monday night alt show, *Eating It*, was "the best place to see comedy in New York City."

The very next evening, on June 1, 1996, Chris Rock's stand-up special *Bring the Pain* debuted on HBO.

As a new generation of comics was creating its own alternative comedy lane, Chris Rock had been grinding it out in old-school comedy clubs across the country. He methodically prepped for his special. It was originally supposed to run thirty minutes, but it got bumped up to an hour after HBO execs caught an early run-through at the Comedy Store.

Rock put everything into this opportunity, working and re-working the material for years. He believed that the '90s black comedy renaissance, kicked off by *In Living Color*, had passed him by. At 31, he felt like a has-been, who had never lived up to his "he's the next Eddie Murphy" hype. Rock had something to prove.

Filmed at the Takoma Theater in Washington, DC, *Bring the Pain* opened with a brazen visual – a montage of comedy album covers: Bill Cosby, Dick Gregory, Flip Wilson, Richard Pryor, Steve Martin, Pigmeat Markham, Woody Allen, and Eddie Murphy.

It was as if Chris Rock was declaring to the world, "I'm next."

Over the next hour, the nerdy kid from Brooklyn unleashed an audacious, provocative, and unflinching performance of a lifetime. Some of the material was so incendiary that, even years later, it was still shocking to hear. And that's precisely what set this special apart, Rock had something to say that no one dared say before.

Bring the Pain garnered Rock two Emmy awards and a Grammy, while catapulting him into the pantheon of stand-up greats. Based on the overwhelmingly positive reaction to his special, HBO gave Rock his own talk and sketch show.

The biggest selling stand-up albums of the era did not come from Chris Rock, Tim Allen, or Martin Lawrence. The comedy record champ was Jeff Foxworthy, thanks to a couple of multi-platinum albums: *You Might Be a Redneck If...* and *Games Rednecks Play*.

Foxworthy, who started at Atlanta's comedy club The Punch-line, had a neat marketing trick – he layered some of his live stand-up routines over a music backing track. That single, entitled "Redneck Stomp," garnered massive play on country radio stations which, in turn, helped drive both album sales and concert tickets.

Adam Sandler used a similar strategy for his albums. Since the days of Redd Foxx and Mort Sahl, most comedy records were live recordings. Not Sandler, his comedy CDs were primarily sketches produced in a recording studio.

That's why it was a pleasant surprise when Sandler had a hit single with a live recording of "The Chanukah Song," captured at UC Santa Barbara. The holiday song helped push his 1996 comedy album, *What The Hell Happened to Me?*, up to #18 on the pop charts and sell over two million copies.

Sandler and Foxworthy's music/comedy convergence echoed earlier musical comedy singles that supported albums like Cheech and Chong's "Basketball Jones" (1973), Steve Martin's "King Tut" (1978), Eddie Murphy's "Boogie in Your Butt" (1982), Rodney Dangerfield's "Rappin' Rodney" (1983), Billy Crystal's "You Look Marvelous" (1985), and Denis Leary's "Asshole" (1993).

Adam Sandler would transcend the world of touring comedy with the successful release of the film, *Billy Madison*. Before the decade was out, the Sandman went on to star in a string of comedy blockbusters including *Happy Gilmore, The Waterboy,* and *The Wedding Singer.*

Stand-ups were getting both airplay and in-house promotion from a mutually beneficial association with radio personalities. Of course, on the road, comedians getting up at dawn to push tickets with a morning radio crew (often called a "zoo") was normal operating procedure. And, early in the comedy boom, San Francisco disc jockey Alex Bennet had actively promoted dozens of local comics. But it was syndicated radio shows from Tom Joyner, Howard Stern, Opie & Anthony, and Bob & Tom that generously championed touring comics. These shows, along with local radio teams such as the Dog House, as well as clip shows like the *5 O'Clock Funnies*, helped a new generation of stand-ups connect with new fans.

Comedy Central eventually found its footing and became a place where young comedians could get early TV exposure and build a career. After some growing pains, the network eventually settled into a farm system of sorts, like a junior HBO. It usually went like this: first a young comic would perform a short set on *Premium Blend* or *Live at Gotham*, then graduate to their own half-hour special (*Comedy Central Presents*), then an hour special. And finally, perhaps, star in their own show on the network. That is the exact path that Demetri Martin, Daniel Tosh, Anthony Jeselnik, and Amy Schumer traveled.

Comedians jumped into animation with the debut of Comedy Central's *Dr. Katz, Professional Therapist.* The brainchild of stand-up comic Jonathan Katz (and Tom Snyder), the show combined low-tech computer animation with some high-wattage comedic talent. Sitting on Katz's therapy couch, and repurposing their stand-up acts, were dozens of comics that helped define the era. They included Ray Romano, Kevin Meaney, Jake Johannsen, Dom Irrera, Laura Kightlinger, Richard Jeni, Rita Rudner, Fred Stoller, Wendy Liebman, Wanda Sykes, John Pinette, Robert Schimmel, and Cathy Ladman.

In 1998, Comedy Central began broadcasting celebrity roasts. A Friars Club tradition dating back to the early 1950s, these raunchy, insult-filled evenings were either behind-closed-doors affairs or cleaned-up versions produced for broadcast television. But as basic cable's obscenity standards loosened, Comedy Central found another avenue to promote, and showcase, comedians.

Stand-ups Bill Maher and Jon Stewart also rose to national fame on Comedy Central with their topical shows *Politically Incorrect* and *The Daily Show*.

Greenwich Village became a comedy hub again as the Comedy Cellar, and its neighbor room, the curiously-named Boston Comedy Club, started attracting crowds. Comics like Kevin Hart, Dave Chappelle, Sarah Silverman, Jay Mohr, Louis C.K., Tracy Morgan, Dave Attell, Todd Barry, Bonnie McFarlane, Bill Burr, Tony Woods, and Bobby Kelly populated the scene.

The Comedy Cellar had a convenient area for comics to congregate post-show, a restaurant directly upstairs from the club called the Olive Tree Cafe. In the corner there was a table reserved exclusively for Cellar comics. The no-holds-barred insult banter at that "comics table" became the template for a new television show hosted by Colin Quinn.

Tough Crowd with Colin Quinn debuted on Comedy Central in 2002. It was a *Politically Incorrect*-type roundtable show that showcased comics engaged in raw, topical debates. *Tough Crowd* showcased Comedy Cellar regulars like Patrice O'Neal, Greg Giraldo, Jim Norton, Rich Vos, Judy Gold, Nick Di Paolo, and Keith Robinson.

Echoing the success of the alt comedy rooms in NYC and L.A., young comics in Chicago created their own scene. Around 2000, venues like the Lyons Den (an open-mic) and the Lincoln Lodge launched the comedic journeys of Hannibal Buress, Kumail Nanjiani, T.J. Miller, Kyle Kinane, Pete Holmes, John Roy, and then later, Cameron Esposito and Beth Stelling.

Chicago-based comic Bernie Mac was on the other side of the comedy spectrum. It wasn't alt rooms or open-mics for Mac. He was able to sell out huge sports arenas, like Madison Square Garden, by combining forces with other headliners.

Comedians Steve Harvey, Cedric the Entertainer, and D.L. Hughley (replacing Guy Torry), joined Mac in a wild, record-setting tour called *The Original Kings of Comedy*. In 2000, director Spike Lee filmed the quartet in Charlotte, North Carolina, and the movie became a runaway hit. It grossed $38 million in theaters and *another* $100 million on home video.

The *Original Kings of Comedy* remains the second highest grossing stand-up concert film in motion picture history. It trails only Eddie Murphy's 1987 film *Raw* (directed by stand-up turned director Robert Townsend).

In its wake, other concert films and specials copied the multiple-act template, giving us *The Queens of Comedy, The Original Latin Kings of Comedy, Blue Collar Comedy Tour, Axis of Evil Comedy Tour,* and *Vince Vaughn's Wild West Comedy Show*.

The '90s presented comedians in films, comedy specials, and sitcoms as never before. As the new century began the world of stand-up was about to change once again, and there were a few early signs of this gathering digital tsunami.

- Rodney Dangerfield was the first comic to a have a personal web site: www.rodney.com
- Touring headliners, like Richard Jeni, started creating huge e-mail lists to directly connect with their fans.
- An internet message board called *ASpecialThing* brought together a community of comedy nerds who chatted about *Mr. Show* and *Tenacious D*. AST also helped popularize *Comedy Death-Ray*, a small weekly L.A. alt show, at the M-Bar, created by Scott Aukerman and BJ Porter.
- Comedian Dane Cook, in 2003, created a personal page on MySpace – a brand-new social networking site. Cook was hoping the site might help promote his shows, drive fans to his website, and maybe sell some online merchandise.

They had no idea what was about to come.

10

DIGITAL DOMAIN

Some people do specials when they've only been doing comedy for three years or something. Which is fine. But I'm kind of old fashioned, and I knew that I didn't want to do one too early.

— ALI WONG

DANE COOK became an unexpected internet pioneer. He was the first comic to successfully augment his stand-up career with an online presence. He invested thousands of dollars on a state-of-the-art custom website and his now-legendary MySpace page became a magnet for new, enthusiastic comedy fans across the country.

Cook spent hours upon hours interacting online with his growing legion of MySpace "friends" (over a million) just as his career shifted into a Steve Martin-esque hyperdrive. Cook sold out sports arenas, appeared on Letterman, starred in both an HBO stand-up series (*Tourgasm*) and a special (*Vicious Circle*), released platinum-selling CDs, landed several starring film roles, graced the cover of *Rolling Stone*, was named one of *Time* magazine's *100 Most Influential People*, and also hosted *Saturday Night Live* – twice.

But Cook was just the beginning.

In the fall of 2004, shooting began on *The Comedians of Comedy* – an alt version of the multi-comic arena movies like *The Original Kings of Comedy*. It followed Zach Galifianakis, Patton Oswalt, Brian Posehn, and Maria Bamford as they struggled through a tour of indie-rock venues. The *Comedians of Comedy* film was the first original content ever financed by a DVD distribution company called Netflix.

In December 2006, a high school junior named Bo Burnham posted an original comedy song entitled *My Whole Family* on YouTube. Burnham's bedroom served as his home TV studio. Within a month the video got millions of hits and suddenly Bo Burnham had a higher profile than thousands of professional comics who had worked the comedy clubs for decades. It was a breathtaking development. A comedian got famous without ever working the clubs (echoing Bob Newhart's 1960 ascent). Two years later, at age 18, Burnham became the youngest comic to tape a Comedy Central special.

Another digital innovation introduced in 2006 was Twitter – a platform that allowed stand-ups to easily and instantly microblog. As smartphones became more ubiquitous over the next several years, comics took to Twitter like cocaine. They began testing jokes, venting about politics, creating virtual fan clubs, selling merchandise, answering questions, providing real-time commentary, or just promoting shows and tours.

Twitter also provided comedy club and theater bookers a new popularity metric: number of followers.

But these new technologies had unforeseen consequences as well. One month before Burnham's song appeared on YouTube, comedian Michael Richards, famous for his portrayal of Cosmo Kramer on *Seinfeld*, launched into a racist improvisational tirade at L.A.'s Laugh Factory. The moment was captured on a customer's cellphone and, when the video aired, Richards' show business career was irreparably damaged.

On February 27, 2005, just as the comedy world was discovering the potential of these new tech innovations, Jamie Foxx was being honored at the Academy Awards. Red Buttons, George Burns, Robin Williams, Whoopi Goldberg, and Mo'Nique had all won Oscars in the Best Supporting actor or actress category. But Jamie Foxx became the first stand-up comic to take home the Best Actor Oscar, for his astonishing portrayal of singer Ray Charles.

Despite the digital wave, stand-up comedy still thrived as an "in-person" experience. No better example was NYC in the early 2000s where venues like Luna Lounge, Rififi, and Pianos provided an array of alt stand-up shows. Fans could catch early sets from Aziz Ansari, Demetri Martin, Chelsea Peretti, Reggie Watts, Jessi Klein, Mike Birbiglia, Jim Gaffigan, H. Jon Benjamin, Kristen Schaal, Kurt Braunohler, and Eugene Mirman.

It was at Rififi, an arm-pit of a room on the Lower East Side, where John Mulaney and Nick Kroll first performed as George St. Geegland and Gil Faizon – two elderly, tuna-obsessed characters that would ultimately bring them to Broadway in *Oh, Hello*.

On both coasts, the Upright Citizens Brigade Theatre, was a critical player in helping to bridge the divide between stand-up, improv, and storytelling. Two UCB shows in particular, L.A.'s *Comedy Death-Ray* (later renamed *Comedy Bang! Bang!*) and NY's *Whiplash*, became prime stand-up bookings. For just a few dollars, and no drink minimums, fans would pack the theater for a chance to see cutting-edge comics.

The UCB shows echoed the economic model of early showcase comedy clubs – there was no pay for the comedians. Yet, most of the acts didn't seem to mind, they jumped at the opportunity to perform in front of enthusiastic, supportive crowds.

These shows allowed comics the freedom to workshop new material, or just bathe in the adoration of a responsive audience.

In June of 2005, Apple updated iTunes to version 4.9, allowing it to support a new medium called podcasts. Now audio content could be easily downloaded or synchronized directly into a player or computer. A few months later, L.A.-based stand-up Jimmy Pardo launched his *Never Not Funny* podcast joining other podcast trailblazers in NYC and London like Keith Malley and Chemda Khalili, Danny Lobell, and Ricky Gervais.

Doug Benson's movie trivia podcast soon followed and the gold rush was on. Podcasts were a creative sandbox for comedians. Comics riffed on sports, getting high, nerd culture, films, murder, depression, politics, music, bizarre news, and the craft of stand-up comedy.

They vented, created characters, role-played, answered questions, improvised, and interrupted each other. Basically, they supercharged the new medium.

There were multiple reasons for the successful comedian / podcast convergence.

1. They were cheap and easy to produce. Podcasts could be recorded at a live venue, or in a living room, car, bedroom, recording studio, or garage.
2. They were an effective promotional tool. Suddenly, just on the juice of a successful podcast, a comedian could tour comedy clubs – and even theaters.
3. Much like the introduction of record albums in the late 1950s, podcasts provided less established acts an entry lane to mainstream success.

4. Advertising dollars or direct Patreon-type support provided some podcasters with a steady revenue stream.

5. Podcasts allowed comedy fans access to the "hang" – the comic's banter-filled world that was previously off-limits.

Marc Maron began his seminal interview podcast, *WTF*, on September 1, 2009. Maron seemed to have a therapist's knack for extracting revealing, intimate details from his guests – primarily other comics. It set the bar for excellence and soon *WTF* became a coveted destination for actors, musicians, writers, directors, and even a sitting U.S. President.

Eventually many podcasts included a companion video feed, frequently on YouTube. This further amplified the reach and impact of their shows. Hours of airtime combined with virtually zero speech restrictions made these new DIY podcast/talk shows extremely compelling and popular.

Comedians also became executives, creating their own podcast networks like Nerdist, Earwolf, All Things Comedy, Corolla Digital, and DeathSquad.

In 2011, comedian Louis C.K. was riding high off the massive critical success of his FX television series *Louie*. He wrote, starred in, and directed every episode of a compelling look into the life of a stand-up comic. During the opening credits, C.K. strolled into NYC's Comedy Cellar. Soon, the Cellar would have to open an auxiliary room, right around the corner, to accommodate the throngs of comedy fans that were flocking to this now iconic venue.

For years C.K. had been creating, performing, and

discarding a new hour of material (he already had starred in specials for HBO, Showtime, and Comedy Central). Then C.K. tried a bold experiment. On December 10, 2011, at noon, his latest stand-up special *Live at the Beacon Theater* became available for downloading exclusively through his website. It cost $5.

C.K.'s gamble turned out to be both successful and groundbreaking. Over 200,000 fans ponied up the money, and eleven days later he had over a million dollars in his PayPal account. Several comedians had already been paid seven figures for their cable specials, so it wasn't the dollar amount that was revolutionary. Louis C.K. demonstrated that comedians could now use the internet to distribute their content directly to fans.

Of course, *Live at the Beacon Theater* was still a digital file that needed to be downloaded, stored, and played off your computer's hard drive. But that too would change as increased broadband speeds and bit rates would hasten the revolution.

Kathy Griffin made some comedy history in 2013 when she broadcast, live on Bravo, her 20th stand-up special. It marked the most specials by any comedian and a representative from Guinness World Records was on hand, in San Antonio, to certify Griffin's accomplishment.

On October 16, 2014, another YouTube video shot by an audience member at a comedy show ignited a storm. The grainy video showed Hannibal Buress's routine about the numerous online rape allegations against stand-up legend Bill Cosby. The following year Cosby was arrested, and then later convicted, on multiple counts of sexual assault. Cosby is currently behind bars in a State Correctional Institution outside Philadelphia, PA.

The proliferation of cell phones, and their video-capturing ability, created a new challenge for touring acts. Some bootleggers would upload a comic's performance, while it was still a work in progress, and post the material online. This activity forced many venues to utilize an invention for the new millennium: cellphone-locking cases.

———

Netflix began producing stand-up specials for streaming in 2013. Their chief content officer, Ted Sarandos, was a self-proclaimed comedy nerd who, during the boom years, often attended Chuckles in Phoenix. But Netflix wasn't the only player in the game: Amazon Prime, Epix, Gumroad, Hulu, Seeso, VHX, Vimeo, and YouTube – along with cable mainstays Comedy Central, HBO, and Showtime – competed in the 21st century stand-up special sweepstakes. When the dust settled, Netflix, because of its immense subscription base, affordability, and ease of use – moved the needle more than any of its rivals.

A successful Netflix special could graduate a comic from clubs to theaters, or from theaters to arenas... just ask John Mulaney or Ali Wong or Bill Burr. Like a successful set on Sullivan or Carson in years past, Netflix became the #1 destination for comics looking to break through.

Then, in 2016, Netflix went all in. It lured Chris Rock away from HBO (Rock had done five HBO specials), plus it also signed up Jerry Seinfeld, Dave Chappelle, Adam Sandler, and Ellen DeGeneres. It showered each comedian with unprecedented multi-million-dollar deals. Adding five comedy legends to its roster helped solidify Netflix's preeminence, while the mind-boggling price tag caused other potential buyers to shiver.

One of those buyers, Seeso, a budding all-comedy streaming service, couldn't compete despite launching right in the middle of the digital boom. They folded just twenty months into their existence. Incredibly, in the same year that Seeso went belly-up (2017), Dave Chappelle released *four* Netflix specials.

Market forces also toppled Turner's Super Deluxe and

caused the perennial comedy website Funny or Die, which had presented the annual traveling *Oddball Comedy and Curiosity Festival*, to scale back its operation. But just as Funny or Die contracted, a new company created their own comedy "lane." Dry Bar used Facebook marketing to help promote their clean, family-friendly content. All of their specials were filmed on a sound stage in Provo, Utah.

Dry Bar wasn't the only player in the *clean comedy* game. PureFlix, a streaming service, found a huge audience when they put up a slate of Christian stand-up specials led by Chondra Pierce. Billing herself as "The Queen of Clean," Pierce tours the country playing to packed crowds in churches, theaters, and civic centers.

Canadian comic Russell Peters, who set multiple international arena attendance records, became a comedy trail-blazer. Inspired by his enormous success, touring overseas became a normal part of a road comic's schedule.

The world was both embracing stand-up comedy and nurturing their own home-grown talent. Multiple think pieces were written about the significance of Hannah Gadsby's breakout 2018 Netflix special, *Nanette*. But largely ignored was the astounding fact that Gadsby was a Tasmanian comedian.

The alt-comedy world has continued to merge into the mainstream. Jonah Ray and Kumail Nanjiani hosted a weekly stand-up show in a converted storage room in the back of an L.A. comic book store. The show became so popular with audiences, *and* comedians, that Comedy Central jumped in and broadcast three seasons of *The Meltdown,* until Jonah and Kumail decided to end the whole thing.

Dozens of themed and specialized comedy nights continue to attract dedicated and delighted fans from Brooklyn to Echo Park. The venues range from music clubs to bars, living rooms, backyards, and converted movie houses (Dynasty Typewriter).

One of the most successful themed shows was called *Roast Battle*. This one-on-one insult competition began in the Comedy Store's tiny Belly Room (originally a female comic only space) and gained a dedicated following. *Roast Battle* rewarded creative joke-writing over stage persona or television credits. The TV-ready format was bought by Comedy Central and even international television versions have spread to the U.K., South Africa, and Mexico.

In its wake, another Belly room success story, *Kill Tony*, has gained a strong following both at the Comedy Store and online. Every week several aspiring comics perform a one-minute set and then face the judgement from a panel of comics led by Tony Hinchcliffe and Brian Redban.

Roast Battle and *Kill Tony* were part of the Comedy Store's stunning resurgence in the 2010s. There were multiple factors that played a role in the club's revival: a new talent booker took over in 2014, two popular Netflix specials were filmed there, and the enormous reach and cultural influence of one comedian's podcast, *The Joe Rogan Experience*.

A five-part Showtime documentary, directed by Mike Binder, explored the Store's massive historical contribution to the world of stand-up comedy.

With a huge number of aspiring comedians populating the entry point of stand-up, the first step onto the comedy ladder was becoming more and more difficult. Most newbies had to endure "bringer shows" where comics were required to provide paying customers in exchange for stage time.

Some open-mics demanded that the comics purchase food or a drink before they were allowed onstage. And in both New York City and Los Angeles, a growing number of *mics* adapted pay-to-play schemes where young comics were charged (cash or Venmo) for the opportunity to perform at a venue/bar. The going rate was $5 for five minutes.

Multiple cultural websites, online magazines, and bloggers were documenting comedy's latest boom. They promoted and reviewed comedy specials, albums, podcasts, casting news, and live dates. Even the *New York Times* was swept up in the wave. For the first time in the paper's 168-year history, they hired a full-time columnist to provide regular "reports from the golden age of comedy."

The internet comedy boom was certainly more inclusive and welcoming to diverse voices from across the human experience. Bob Smith, back in 1994, was the first openly gay comic to appear on the *Tonight Show*. Twenty-three years later, in 2017, Jaboukie Young-White came out to his parents during his first *Tonight Show* set.

Comedy festivals like Montreal's *Just For Laughs* were thriving, while new ones sprouted up all over the United States (Iowa had two). Most major music festivals included a comedy venue or tent. In San Francisco, Comedy Central presented a "colossal" comedy festival entitled *Clusterfest*.

At the start of 2018, there were three television series that dramatized the lives of comedians: Showtime's *I'm Dying Up Here*, HBO's *Crashing*, and Amazon's breakout hit *The Marvelous Mrs. Maisel*.

The heights of the comedy boom were stunning.

- Kevin Hart sold out a football stadium: Philadelphia's Lincoln Financial Field.
- Dave Chappelle did a 16-night "residency" at a small comedy room called Radio City Music Hall.
- Sebastian Maniscalco performed four shows over a single weekend at Madison Square Garden, grossing a jaw-dropping $8.28 million dollars for his Friday/Saturday gig.

The list of comics who can sell out MSG grows every year. But the boom was not just confined to acts at the top of the pyramid. A growing circuit of medium-sized theaters and music clubs were filling their calendars with stand-up headliners. Plus, traditional '80s-style two-drink-minimum comedy clubs still flourished in multiple cities.

There were numerous stand-up-only satellite radio stations that featured programming across a spectrum of comedic preferences: clean, explicit, urban, blue collar, and even Canadian. SoundExchange, which collects and distributes royalties from audio streamers and digital radio, became a financial Santa Claus to thousands of 21st century comedians.

YouTube became a powerful option for comics looking to release their own full-length stand-up specials. Sam Morril, Mark Normand, and Joe List's straight-to-YouTube specials generated millions of views and a slew of new fans.

Three universities and colleges, most notably Emerson, now offer comedy nerds a fully accredited bachelor's degree program in comedic arts. Perhaps Albert Brooks, who satirized the idea of a "School for Comedians" back in 1971 in *Esquire* magazine, could give the commencement address.

CNN, a news channel, debuted its first stand-up special, Colin Quinn's *Red State Blue State*.

And, as if that wasn't enough, the National Comedy Center, complete with Jim Gaffigan hologram and a place for George Carlin's "stuff," opened in Jamestown, New York.

Then, in March 2020, the COVID-19 pandemic stopped it all in its tracks.

Comedy clubs and theaters were among the first businesses to shut down and will probably be among the last to fully reopen. Humans inside, laughing out loud, with close-packed seating and low ceilings were ideal conditions for great stand-up comedy, as well as the transmission of airborne viruses.

Stand-up comedian Jacqueline Novak spent years creating her one-woman show, *Get on Your Knees*. After a successful run in New York City, she was booked on a 2020 theater tour of the US and Europe. Then, it all vanished as the world struggled to contain the virus.

Novak was not alone. Tom Segura, Nikki Glaser, Jo Koy, Bert Kreisher, Whitney Cummings, Jim Jefferies, Iliza Shlesinger, Gabriel Iglesias, Roy Wood Jr., Nate Bargatze and hundreds of other touring comics were all in the same boat. Even Eddie Murphy's long-awaited return to stand-up in 2020 was put on hold.

Optimistic comics first rescheduled their dates to late summer 2020, and then to the fall, and then to spring 2021. No one knew when it would end.

COVID-19 restrictions varied county by county. Various cities still allowed *some* indoor comedy shows to soldier on with a creative array of modifications: limited seating capacity, mask use, plexiglass between tables, or making comics use separate microphones – that they'd have to disconnect after their set.

New Yorkers were extremely resourceful repurposing some indoor spaces, without liquor licenses, to host stand-up events. Shows were held in churches, and quasi-churches, because religious institutions were partially exempt from social gathering rules.

Some comedians decided to wait it out until it was completely safe to tour. But others, like a Mickey Rooney/Judy Garland plotline, were determined to put on a show. Even if it meant performing from the back of a U-Haul.

And so, a new era of live stand-up comedy began. There were three primary options for fans to catch shows during the pandemic.

OUTDOORS

The outside option transformed public parks, backyards, patios, courtyards, parking lots, and rooftops as makeshift stand-up venues. There was a guerilla theater aspect to these pop-up shows. They were sometimes illegal and always a health risk. On occasion, law enforcement shut them down.

Most outdoor shows used portable microphone systems but a few went old-school amplification-free comedy. There wasn't much pay, contribution buckets were passed around or funds were transferred to Venmo accounts. But soon both promoters and comedy clubs stepped in and augmented the budding outdoor DIY scene with ticketed admissions.

Netflix postponed, and then cancelled, its inaugural *Netflix Is a Joke* festival in Los Angeles, but somehow Dave Chappelle managed to produce his own mini festival near his home in Ohio.

For a few months in 2020, the city of Yellow Springs became the nation's stand-up mecca. *Dave Chappelle & Friends: An Intimate Socially Distanced Affair* presented an all-star lineup of comics that included Michelle Wolf, Chris Rock, Jon Stewart, Tiffany Haddish, Michael Che, Brian Regan, Louis C.K., Chris Tucker, Trevor Noah, Mo Amer, Ali Wong, Kevin Hart, Bill Burr, Donnell Rawlings, and even David Letterman.

Netflix crews documented the goings-on in what became known as "Chappelle's Summer Camp." Every show was sold out, drawing audiences from all over the country, until concerns about the virus shut the whole thing down.

AUTOMOBILES / SUBWAYS

"Drive in" comedy in parking lots sprung up as a smart way to keep audience members safe and isolated. Fans paid a *per car* cover charge and the comic's audio was broadcast over FM radio. Positive audience feedback was delivered in the form of flashing headlights or car horns.

In New York City, when the winter weather drove audiences out of parks and off the rooftops, one work-around was utilizing the last car of the Seventh Avenue local subway. For the first time ever, the #1 train was transformed into a rolling comedy club.

ONLINE

Zoom, Instagram Live, YouTube, Facebook Live, and Twitch became the primary platforms used to stream live stand-up during the pandemic. It was the safest option. The playing field was leveled somewhat as both headliners and open-mic'ers struggled with the technology's challenges and limitations.

The primary drawback with digital streaming was its inability to replicate the *immediate audience reaction* which lies at the heart of live comedy. Comedian Dana Gould once described stand-up as, "A conversation – but only one person is talking."

It was difficult for comics to get on a roll when the only feedback were emojis of hands clapping or LOLs typed into a scrolling chat window. One work-around was cherry-picking enthusiastic laughers from the online audience and unmuting their audio.

A whole generation of performers had come of age in a live/digital hybrid comedy world, and their transition to online shows was not as daunting. In fact, for some, it seemed like the logical next step.

In a few areas, streaming stand-up had unique advantages over in-person shows. For example:

- Comedians, from their bedroom, could now perform live shows for audiences across the globe.
- Realtime tipping was a nice bonus.
- A gallery view on Zoom could be helpful for crowd work.
- Superfans were willing to pay a premium for post-show meet & greets, Q&As, or photo opportunities.
- Popular themed shows (*Hot Tub*, *UnCabaret*, *Cabernet Cabaret*) could now be enjoyed by a wider audience outside of their origin city.

Companies like RushTix, Bonfire, House Seats, NoWhere Comedy Club, and HoldThePhone quickly moved into the streaming marketplace. They were able to promote, produce, and monetize shows for comedians with large fan bases, or for comics who teamed up for multi-act "concept" nights. Maybe the biggest corporate winner (besides Zoom) was Eventbrite, the online ticketing service.

Even before the pandemic arrived, there was already a popular genre of performers known as front-facing comedians. They used their smartphone cameras to create intimate virtual content.

These remarkable videos were able to showcase an aspiring comic's talents in the most direct way yet imagined. Why create a whole web series when you can boil down your comedy, acting, and writing skills using just a phone and Instagram, Twitter, or TikTok? It was another dramatic example of how comics continue to exploit technological opportunities. And it's already paying huge dividends.

During the shutdown, Sarah Cooper, a lip-sync artist

(exactly how Jerry Lewis started) became an online phenomenon and got signed for a Netflix special *and* a CBS sitcom. While Ziwe Fumudoh signed on to create, and host, a new variety show on Showtime.

Ziwe is a perfect example of a 21st century hybrid comedian – equally comfortable performing on stage at Brooklyn Hall or streaming her interview show using Instagram Live.

SOME FINAL THOUGHTS

How the acceleration of online streaming will change stand-up comedy is anyone's guess. Perhaps digital content will become the dominant comedic force leaving live stand-up comedy as a quaint, old-timey curiosity. A relic from another century. Or, maybe, when fans get the chance to *go out* and experience the juice of a live in-person performance, they will view digital comedy as a pale doppelgänger.

Whatever the answer is, the next stand-up comedy historian will chronicle that story.

We know that, since the late 1800s, comedians have adapted to new technologies. Yet performing live, alone on stage, remains the defining aspect of the profession. That terrifying-to-thrilling experience, in front of an audience, is what connects stand-up comedians through time.

So, whether its Artemus Ward, Bob Hope, Jack Benny, Lenny Bruce, Phyllis Diller, Rickles, Dangerfield, Pryor, Carlin, Rivers, Rock, Cho, Oswalt, Silverman, Burr, Schumer, or Chappelle.

They all do the same thing.

In one.

HISTORY OF STAND-UP TIMELINE

1861 Nov. 26 - Artemus Ward performs his first comedy lecture. Lawrence Hall in New London, Connecticut.

1888 May 12 - Marshall P. Wilder delivers the first comedy monologue ever recorded. Electric Club, NYC.

1895 July - Mark Twain begins his world comedy tour with 22 dates in North America.

1906 June 4 - Bert Williams releases "Nobody" for Columbia. It is the first pre-1920 recording inducted into the Grammy Hall of Fame.

1908 May - 16-year-old Eddie Cantor wins amateur night competition at Miner's Bowery Theatre. $5 first prize.

1910 June 20 - Comic-singer Fanny Brice makes her *Ziegfeld Follies* debut.

1913 March 24 - Vaudeville's Palace Theater opens. Ed Wynn is the first comedian to perform on its stage.

1913 - Joe Hayman records "Cohen On the Telephone." First comedy record to sell a million copies.

1923 - Jackie Mabley (later to add "Moms") makes her NYC debut at the Harlem nightclub, Connie's Inn.

1926 May 30 - Will Rogers becomes the first comedian to perform political material on stage with a current US President (Woodrow Wilson) in attendance.

1932 May 2 - Jack Benny's radio show debuts. It runs for 23 seasons.

1936 Dec. 10 - Fred Allen accidentally kicks off a friendly, and popular, radio feud with Jack Benny.

1940 Feb. 29 - Bob Hope hosts the Academy Awards for the first time.

1940 Nov. 30 - Minnie Pearl makes her debut on WSM's *Grand Ole Opry*.

1945 - Jean Carroll tries stand-up comedy.

1946 July 25 - Dean Martin and Jerry Lewis team up at the Atlantic City nightclub, Club 500.

1948 June 23 - Variety first uses the term "stand-up" to describe a specific style of comedy.

1949 May 16 - Milton Berle, host of NBC's *Texaco Star Theater,* graces the cover of both *Time* magazine and *Newsweek*.

1949 Sep. 25 - Stand-up/impressionist George Kirby becomes the first African American comic to do a set on *Toast of The Town* (later rebranded *The Ed Sullivan Show*).

1953 Oct. 2 - Victor Borge brings his act to Broadway and proceeds to set the record for longest running one-man show.

1953 Dec. 22 - Mort Sahl debuts at San Francisco's hungry i.

1954 Sep. 27 - *The Tonight Show* begins its historic run on NBC. It is first hosted by Steve Allen.

1956 - Redd Foxx releases the comedy album, *Laff of The Party*, on Dooto Records

1957 April - Timmie Rogers becomes the first stand-up to headline the Apollo Theater.

1959 Jan. - Shelley Berman's debut album, *Inside Shelly Berman*, is released. First stand-up album to win a Grammy.

1959 May - Insult comedian Don Rickles begins working the Casbar lounge at the Sahara Hotel in Las Vegas.

1959 July 13 - *Time* magazine publishes a critical take-down of the newest style of comedians: The Sickniks.

1960 May 6 - *The Button-Down Mind of Bob Newhart* is released. Wins Record of the Year. #1 album in USA for 14 weeks.

1961 Jan. - Dick Gregory helps break the nightclub color line and becomes the first African American stand-up headliner at Chicago's Playboy Club.

1961 Oct. 4 - Lenny Bruce, in San Francisco, is arrested for uttering an obscenity on stage.

1964 - Dave Astor is the first stand-up comic to perform at The Improvisation Café in NYC.

1965 Feb. 17 - Joan Rivers makes her debut on *The Tonight Show starring Johnny Carson*.

1967 Feb. 5 - *The Smothers Brothers Comedy Hour* begins on CBS.

1968 Jan. 22 - *Rowan and Martin's Laugh-In* begins on NBC.

1972 Jan. 31 - Flip Wilson is featured on the cover of *Time* magazine. "TV's First Black Superstar."

1972 April 7 - Comic Sammy Shore, wife Mitzi, and writer Rudy DeLuca open The Comedy Store. L.A.'s first comedy club.

1972 May 1 - Johnny Carson moves *The Tonight Show* from New York City to Los Angeles.

1973 Dec. 12 - Freddie Prinze, just 19 years old, makes his stunning debut on *The Tonight Show*.

1975 Oct. 11 - George Carlin hosts the inaugural broadcast of NBC's *Saturday Night*.

1975 Dec. 31 - Robert Klein headlines the first HBO stand-up special. Taped at Haverford College.

1976 April 26 - HBO broadcasts the prototype "young comedians special" from the Hollywood Improv w/ Freddie Prinze.

1977 March 24 - Lily Tomlin opens on Broadway in *Appearing Nitely*. Receives a special Tony Award.

1977 Oct. - Steve Martin releases his first comedy album, *Let's Get Small*. Recorded at the Boarding House.

1977 Oct. 20 - Native American stand-up Charlie Hill makes his network debut on NBC's *The Richard Pryor Show*.

1978 April 3 - Woody Allen's 1977 film *Annie Hall* takes home Oscars for Best Picture, Original Screenplay, and Directing.

1978 July 3 - U.S. Supreme Court rules 5-4 in *FCC v. Pacifica* that the government can prohibit radio broadcasts that contain indecent language (re: George Carlin's "Filthy Words" from the album *Occupation: Foole*).

1979 Jan. 5 - The first stand-up film, *Richard Pryor: Live in Concert*, is released to critical acclaim.

1979 Jan. 22 - David Letterman guest-hosts *The Tonight Show* just two months after his *Tonight Show* stand-up debut.

1983 Aug. 17 - Eddie Murphy's mega stand-up special, *Delirious*, debuts on HBO.

1985 Aug. 3 - Sam Kinison performs on HBO's *9th Annual Young Comedians Special*, hosted by Rodney Dangerfield.

1986 March 29 - Robin Williams, Whoopi Goldberg, and Billy Crystal host the *Comic Relief* telethon/benefit.

1986 Dec. 22 - Jackie Mason's solo show, *The World According to Me!*, is a hit on Broadway. Receives a special Tony award.

1988 Oct. 18 - *Roseanne* debuts on ABC.

1990 Feb. 21 - Andrew "Dice" Clay becomes the first comic to sell out Madison Square Garden.

1991 Aug. - Janeane Garofalo and friends kick-start the modern alt-comedy scene at Big & Tall Books in Los Angeles.

1992 - Bernie Mac declares "I ain't scared of you mother...." " on HBO's *Def Comedy Jam*.

1992 Aug. 15 - *The Larry Sanders Show* co-created and starring Garry Shandling debuts on HBO.

1992 Oct. 1 - Bill Hicks performs on *The Late Show with David Letterman*. His set is removed before the broadcast.

1993 Nov. - Beth Lapides brings *UnCabaret* to LunaPark in West Hollywood.

1994 - Jim Carrey stars in three comedy blockbusters in the same calendar year: *Pet Detective, The Mask,* and *Dumb and Dumber*.

1994 Sept. 14 - Stand-up Margaret Cho stars in *All-American Girl* – the first sitcom to feature an Asian American family.

1994 Nov. - Tim Allen holds the #1 TV show, #1 movie, and #1 book - all in the same week.

1995 July 18 - Jeff Foxworthy comedy album *Games Rednecks Play* is released. It goes triple platinum.

1996 May 31 - *The New York Times* declares alt show *Eating It* as "the best place to see comedy in New York City."

1996 June 1 - Chris Rock's HBO special, *Bring the Pain*, airs.

1999 Jan. 11 - Jon Stewart takes over *The Daily Show* from Craig Kilborn, ushering in a new political comedy era.

2000 Aug. 18 - *The Original Kings of Comedy* film is released w/ Steve Harvey, Cedric the Entertainer, D.L. Hughley, Bernie Mac.

2000 Oct. 15 - *Curb Your Enthusiasm* starts its run on HBO w/ Larry David, Jeff Garlin, Susie Essman.

2003 Dec. - Dane Cook creates his MySpace page.

2004 - First original content financed by Netflix, *The Comedians of Comedy*, begins filming.

2005 Feb. 27 - Jamie Foxx wins Best Actor at the Oscars.

2005 Aug. 12 - *The Aristocrats* is released. A documentary that examines a single joke. Directed by Paul Provenza and Penn Jillette.

2005 Nov. 28 - Carrot Top (Scott Thompson) begins his record-setting residency at the Luxor Hotel in Las Vegas.

2006 Nov. 9 - Bill Burr unleashes an epic takedown of the city of Philadelphia, after a crowd boos Dom Irrera off the stage.

2006 Dec. 21 - Bo Burnham uploads his original song, "My Whole Family," on YouTube.

2007 Jan. - Anjelah Johnson's "Nail Salon" debuts on YouTube.

2009 July 4 - Larry the Cable Guy (aka Dan Whitney) performs for over 55,000 fans at a football stadium in Nebraska.

2009 Sept. 1 - Marc Maron begins his *WTF* podcast.

2009 Nov. 9 - George Lopez is the first Mexican American to host a late-night talk show on an English-speaking network.

2010 - Kumail Nanjiani and Jonah Ray begin *The Meltdown with Jonah and Kumail* in the back room of an L.A. comic book store.

2011 Dec. 11 – Louis C.K. distributes *Live at the Beacon Theater* from his personal website.

2012 Aug. 3 - Tig Notaro opens her set at Largo with, "Hello, I have cancer," just four days after her diagnosis. A recording of the performance is later released.

2015 Aug. 30 - Kevin Hart sells out a football stadium in Philadelphia.

2016 May 5 - Ali Wong's Netflix special *Baby Cobra* debuts.

2018 Mar. 27 - James Acaster debuts 4-part *Repertoire* on Netflix.

2018 June 19 - Netflix releases Hannah Gadsby's *Nanette,* sparking a debate about the nature of stand-up.

2019 Jan. 19/20 - Sebastian Maniscalco plays four shows, over two nights at Madison Square Garden. Grosses $8.2 million.

2020 Jan. 5 - At the Golden Globes, Ramy Youseef receives Best Actor in a Comedy Series for *Ramy.*

ACKNOWLEDGMENTS

First and foremost, I'm indebted to Megh Wright and Jesse Fox at *Vulture*. Without their initial encouragement, I would still be talking, and not writing, about stand-up's history.

My brain trust of comedy history experts: Ritch Shydner, Kliph Nesteroff, Katie Mears, Neal Brennan, Robert Bader, Dana Gould, Jeff Abraham, Stephen J. Morrison, and Dan Pasternack.

The people who helped edit this book: Joe Bolster, Jennifer Rose, Alex Gootter, Wayne Jones, and Rob Ross.

Publicists Jess Guinivan and Greg Longstreet.

My crews at USC Comedy and School of Dramatic Arts: Dean Elizabeth Daly, David Isaacs, Barnet Kellman, Jack Epps, Justin Wilson, Alex Ago, J. D. Connor, Brian DeAngelis, Lori Ray, Kirstin Eggers, Judith Shelton, Zachary Steel, and David Bridel, the person who hired me.

My podcasting partners: Andrew Steven and Jeff Umbro.

And especially: Saraphina Monaco, Dave Rath, Judd Apatow, Ron Bennington, Journey Gunderson, Mark Flanagan, Jordan Brady, Josh Church, Adam Ray, Marlene Vigil, Barry Weintraub, Mike Rowe, Kathryn Busby, Matt McGough, Jimmy Fallon, Kate Stockrahm, Tom Papa, Brandon Mullins, Illeana Douglas, Dave Becky, Jimmy Miller, Geno Michellini, Barry Katz, Jake Kroeger, Wendy Wilkins, Jennifer Heftler, Jeff Garlin, Marc Hershon, Carol Ann Leif, John Fugelsang, Jamie Flam, Vanessa Ragland, and Greg Fitzsimmons.

Also, the late Phil Berger.

BIBLIOGRAPHY

Allen, Fred *Much Ado About Me*. Little, Brown and Co. 1956

Allen, Steve *The Funny Men*. Simon and Schuster 1956

Apatow, Judd *Sick in the Head*. Random House 2015

Berger, Phil *The Last Laugh*. William Morrow 1975

Forbes, Camille F. *Introducing Bert Williams*. Basic Civitas 2008

Foxx, Redd, Miller, Norma *Encyclopedia of Black Humor*. W. Ritchie Press 1977

Hendra, Tony *Going Too Far*. Dolphin Books 1987

Knoedelseder, William *I'm Dying Up Here*. PublicAffairs 2009

Laurie Jr., Joe *From Vaude to Video*. Henry Holt 1951

Lax, Eric *On Being Funny*. Charterhouse 1975

Martin, Steve *Born Standing Up*. Scribner 2007

Murrells, Joseph *Million Selling Records*. Arco 1985

Nachman, Gerald *Seriously Funny*. Back Stage Books, 2004

Nesteroff, Kliph *The Comedians*. Grove Press, 2015

Oswalt, Patton *Silver Screen Fiend*. Scribner 2015

Parish, James Robert, Leonard William *The Funsters*. 1979

Paar, Jack *My Saber is Bent*. Trident Press 1961

S.D., Trav *No Applause, Just Throw Money*. Faber and Faber 2005

Saul, Scott *Becoming Richard Pryor*. Harper Collins 2005

Shydner, Ritch *Kicking Through the Ashes*. Mr. Media Books 2016

Watkins, Mel *On the Real Side*. Lawrence Hill Books 1999

Wilde, Larry *The Great Comedians Talk About Comedy*. Lyle Stewart 1973

Zinoman, Jason *Letterman*. Harper Collins 2017

Zoglin, Richard *Comedy at the Edge*. Bloomsbury USA, 2009

Zweibel, Alan *Laugh Lines*. Abrams Press 2020

INDEX

ABOUT THE AUTHOR

1979 Raquette Lake, New York

Wayne Federman is a stand-up, actor, author, professor, musician, and podcaster. Wayne has been a touring stand-up comedian for over 35 years and has appeared multiple times on *The Tonight Show*. He has his own special on Comedy Central and will soon release another special, *Live at The World Theater*. Wayne co-produced the Emmy-winning documentary *The Zen Diaries of Garry Shandling* and is co-producing the new George Carlin documentary for HBO.

Wayne has acted in numerous films and TV shows including *Legally Blonde, Knocked Up, Step Brothers, The 40−Year−Old Virgin, 50 First Dates, Funny People, Curb Your Enthusiasm, Silicon Valley, Shameless, The Larry Sanders Show, Community, Living Single,* and *The X-Files*. Wayne co-wrote the sports bestseller MARAVICH The *Authorized biography of Pistol Pete.* ("The definitive biography of Pete Maravich" ESPN). He currently co-hosts the acclaimed podcast: *The History of Stand-Up*, and is an adjunct professor of stand-up history at USC.

He lives in Los Angeles.

WayneFederman.com
  twitter - @Federman
  instagram - @InstaFederman